COLOSSAL CONSIDERATIONS

THOUGHT-PROVOKING INSIGHTS TO MOVE YOUR LIFE FORWARD

BY RONNIE DOSS

WWW.RONNIEDOSS.COM

Preface

I wrote this book for YOU! I know you are busy, and I know there are people that depend on you. Every single day, we have a chance to get up and begin again with a little more knowledge and a little more experience than we had the day before. The insights in this book are meant to get you thinking about where you are, where you want to go, and what you want to become. I recommend reading one of these considerations per day and meditating on it throughout the day. Look for ways to implement the considerations into your life and notice how things begin to change. One thought, one idea, and one action step can change everything for you. Don't rush through the book. Pick it up and read just a little at a time. Discuss what you are learning with the people closest to you. Ask for people to share their perspectives on the considerations with you. The book is simply meant to be a catalyst for better thinking. I hope you enjoy what I have shared, and I pray that you believe in yourself enough to pursue the things you once believed were impossible.

You are worth the work! Let's go.

1

A Work vs. THE Work

"Working on yourself is the best investment you will ever make. It will profoundly improve your life and positively impact the lives of those around you."

Ronnie Doss

Going to your job is doing "A work." Knocking out a to-do list is also doing "A work." Doing "THE work" is when you focus on expanding your thinking and breaking through old belief patterns that may keep you stuck in unhealthy patterns. Getting older is easy; getting better requires doing "THE work." You're already dead if you aren't reading new things, listening to new things, experiencing new things, and learning new ways of experiencing yourself. Notice what you're thinking and feeling as you do "A work," and you can develop much more self-awareness and make adjustments to what you are doing with your creative energy. "THE work" is about becoming more than you already are by paying attention in ways you never have. Focusing on your internal chatter and asking yourself why you speak to yourself the way you do can be a great starting point for changing your attitude and energy. Could today be the day you begin doing "THE work" on yourself and refining your self-talk? If so, doing "THE work" that we will discuss throughout this book will be the most exciting and fulfilling thing you've ever done. "THE work" can unlock things about you that you haven't considered, and those new realizations can transform how you live your life.

2

Play SMALL, And Everyone LOSES

"When you neglect your dreams, it becomes a mental disease that will infect your mind and diminish your power."

Ronnie Doss

The world needs you! YOU need you! When you refuse to take your rightful place as a leader, the people looking for a solid model to follow miss out. Winners play big, losers play small. Your family is waiting to see you excel. Your friends are hoping you will excel. Humanity needs you to excel. It's time to step up or step off. It's GO time for the ones courageous enough to enter the arena. There is a difference between "playing to win" and "playing not to lose." Can you think of one area of your life that you have allowed yourself to play small? If so, what will you begin doing today to start playing big again? What dream do you need to awaken? What discipline will you develop? Who will benefit besides you when you dig in and stop cowering to your fears? The time is NOW! Your future self will thank you. The people you are here to serve will thank you. Play big and make yourself proud!

3

Meanings For MATURITY

"Life is not about what happens to us. Life is about what we tell ourselves regarding what happens to us."

Ronnie Doss

Maturity is when we take ownership of our stories and create emotions that serve us and the people who will interact with us. Emotions follow focus, and focus is a choice. So, the emotions we experience have much to do with what we choose to focus on. Getting control of your focus and the story you create about what you see is one of the most profound shifts you can ever make regarding your emotional and mental well-being. No one can do this work for you; that is why it is so important. Change is an inside-out job. The next time you start overreacting to a situation, ask yourself, "Why am I choosing this perspective?" The instant you realize that you can change the narrative on any event is the moment you take your power back. What is a story you have about made up about yourself that is causing you to feel disempowered? Is it your family status? Is it your financial status? Do you feel underqualified for something you want to achieve? How would your outlook on the future change if you began rewriting the narrative you've created about yourself up to this point? You can be excited again! Create the story to make that happen NOW, and continue practicing that story until it becomes your truth.

4

DENIAL Is A COCOON That SUFFOCATES Our POTENTIAL

"Denial can be a seductive companion, but the price you must pay is huge. Denial sneaks its way into your life and will cripple you before too long."

Ronnie Doss

Many people are too alive to die but too dead to live. "Semi-lazy" is a term used to describe the people who do just enough to get by so they don't appear lazy to others. When you live in denial, you're simply avoiding a truth that only you know may be painful to admit. When you face your problems, they get smaller; when you run from them, they get bigger. All of us have areas that we can improve upon. All of us are falling short in some place or another. Denial is not the key; it is the lock that can keep you in a frustrated prison for much of your life. If you want out of the prison, be honest about the fact that you are in one. Next, ask for some accountability and begin taking action toward the solution. If you have to, put some risk into the game. Put a date and time stamp on your action step and have someone hold you accountable. For example, give your trusted person a written check to mail to your least favorite political party if you don't follow the action steps. Maybe they send the money to an organization you disagree with. Perhaps the money goes anonymously to someone you don't like. No matter what, nothing changes if nothing changes. What is something about yourself that you've been in denial about that is keeping you from feeling and doing your best? Who could you ask for support to help you address it and take action? You may be fooling everyone else, but you can't fool yourself.

5

EMBRACING UNCERTAINTY

"Certainty is the fast road to a mediocre life."

Ronnie Doss

If you have to control everything, you will eventually have little left to control. In professional settings, micromanaging and control can quickly become a poison that creates a toxic work environment. In personal relationships, control takes the form of coercion and manipulation. No one wants to be in a relationship like that. Our current world is changing at a faster rate than ever before. Your mind is continually bombarded with information that can distract you from your purpose and minimize your effectiveness. If you're going to control anything, control only the controllable things. The controllable things are your thinking, mental and physical diet, movement, and environment. Everything else is out of your control. So, do what you can with things that are the highest priority and let the rest go. What area have you been trying to control that, if you "surrendered it" and trusted the process, would improve the quality of your mental and emotional well-being? Is there someone you owe an apology to for trying to control or manipulate them? Embrace the uncertainty and free yourself from the bondage of control.

6
UNATTACHED vs. DETACHED

"Detachment eventually leads to a life of quiet desperation. Humans are social beings, and our well-being is intricately connected to the fabric of human connection."

Ronnie Doss

There are lots of bad things happening in the world. We can see what is happening and create solutions when we remain UNATTACHED. Being DETACHED means we are clueless about what is happening around us because we are only focused on ourselves. When I think of being detached, I envision an individual tucked away in their basement playing a video game with zero understanding of what is happening in the real world. People become detached from relationships, teams, family, and potential contributions when they are unwilling to pay attention to problems that may be negatively affecting their lives and the lives of others. Yes, atrocities are happening in the world, but that does not mean we should become detached. Leaders are emotionally unattached to adverse circumstances that may be occurring around them and, at the same time, are willing to contribute to the solution. When you remain unattached, you can see solutions more clearly than if you allow yourself to become blinded by the intense impulses of emotion. Be creative in how you can be part of a solution while keeping your personal goals and vision as a high priority. It can be both! You have much more capacity than you think, so don't detach from life simply because it is chaotic and challenging. Step up, step in, and serve with the ideas you have and the resources you have available to you. The world needs you more than you know.

7
HEARING vs. LISTENING

"Many people do not listen to hear what the other person hopes to convey. People typically listen to find a place to interject their opinion."

Ronnie Doss

We hear people talk all day. Social media outlets, mass media outlets, and day-to-day conversations are happening all around us. For our relationships to grow deeper, we must develop a more profound sense of awareness of what other people are saying. Silence can often do much of the heavy lifting in robust conversations. We must learn to listen to what is not told while paying attention to the spoken words. We must move out of our heads and into the deeper parts of our being to do this. The greatest gift you can give someone is your undivided attention. Moving forward, I challenge you to ask more and more questions as you go throughout your day. Try to be more interested than interesting. When someone shares something with you, ask them to tell you more about what they are discussing. Use phrases like "That's interesting" and "I'd like to understand more about that." Which of your relationships would improve if you were willing to improve your listening skills and ask better questions? Ask your way into the next level of relationships and see how far you can go. Remember, listening isn't just about your ears. Listening is about your heart.

Obsession With An
UNRESOLVED PAST

"Take an axe to any tree that provides bad fruit, even if you planted it yourself."

Ronnie Doss

Take a moment to consider your job, your friend group, and your business partners. Do those relationships help you to produce good things? Do they cause you to level up in your life? We often get caught up in circumstances that no longer serve us or our future. When you continually assess your situations and surroundings, you can evaluate whether things benefit you. You can love people from a distance. You can be friendly to people without being friends with everyone. There is nothing wrong with setting boundaries and choosing to distance yourself from things that are unhealthy for you. Remember, what you tolerate continues to exist. If you want better, you must choose better. Pull up the weeds before they take over your garden. Cut down the tree that produces bad fruit. Cut off the relationships that drain you. Stop the behavior that is destroying you. You are **worth the work**.

BROKEN MACHINES STILL PRODUCE

"Your days are very limited, so never allow yourself to waste them because of indecision. Decide to decide and then move forward with boldness."

Ronnie Doss

It's never about one particular action step that changes our lives, but rather a collection of actions that produce patterns. Patterns are what lead to long-lasting consequences. When we neglect the changes we need to make, we develop habits, and habits lead to our destiny. Yes, you can get away with most things for a while, but without making the necessary changes to stay on the right path, you can die from a thousand little cuts. Those cuts become deep wounds that can infect your life severely. What is a pattern that you have fallen into that needs to change? What are the consequences of not changing, and what damage could those consequences do to others? You are going to produce something, whether you are intentional or not. Taking the time to design your days versus defaulting into your days will make all the difference in the world. Finishing your day in your mind before you even begin your day is a wonderful way to gain some direction and be more effective and efficient with your energy.

10

The Struggle Is REAL, So Are The RESULTS

"Strength is developed right in the middle of the struggle. If you run from the struggle, you run from your strength."

Ronnie Doss

To create powerful results in any endeavor, we must be willing to get comfortable with being uncomfortable. If an individual can't handle stress, they will not be able to handle success. People committed to growth understand that it all comes with a price. Comfort leads to complacency and casualness. We lose our strength if we continually put ourselves in situations requiring no effort. Your brain is a muscle; you must work to make it stronger. The best way to make yourself more robust and equipped for success is to put yourself into situations that provide intentional tension. Dealing with tension will strengthen your stamina and increase your resolve. You get stronger mentally and physically when you push yourself through the tension. Individuals who refuse to deal with stress will never create great success. Some say that sweat is a weakness leaving the body, but I believe mediocrity is also going. What tension are you intentionally immersing yourself into currently? Are you pushing yourself or procrastinating? Remember, both will produce a result. You must choose which one you are most committed to.

11

The PRIZE FIGHT Will Always Be With YOURSELF

"When you finally recognize that the only person you should compete with is your former self, you free yourself from being a victim to what others may or may not be doing."

Ronnie Doss

Our society runs on highlight reels. Social media is a platform for everyone to show how well their life works but rarely displays their struggles. Social media portrays only a fraction of what is going on in people's lives. If you compare your entire life to someone else's highlight reel, you will always feel like you are losing. If you want to win the fight, you must win the battle of focus. What you focus on will continue to expand so long as you continue to give it the thing that gives it its power: your attention! Your attention gives things their power, so why not focus on the things within you that will help you grow stronger? If you conquer the enemy inside of you, all other enemies can not harm you. Look within **you**. Look at the gifts you have to bring to the fight. Choose your battles wisely. Not everything is worthy of your attention. Conserve your energy by focusing on the things that will help you win. Falling into the comparison trap is one thing that can tap large amounts of your energy. Evaluate how much time you spend on social media and think about how much sharper you'd be if you were to train your body and mind for success. Before too long, you can be far ahead of the crowd with the right amount of personal management. You're a champion; act like it!

12

If You Take The Easy Road, You'll Wind Up HITCHHIKING The Rest Of YOUR LIFE

"Nothing that is easy lasts and will never make you proud."

Ronnie Doss

The most challenging things you do with your life will inevitably produce what you are most proud of. If you take the easy road, eventually, you will have to beg to get somewhere better. There is a time and place for everything, and moderation is good. However, if you continue only to do things that are "easy," you will eventually have to beg for things that others have achieved through discipline. There are two roads: the high road and the easy road. The high road has much less traffic because few people choose to take it. But, the people who take it move faster toward their destiny. The other road is the easy road. The easy road leads to poverty, lack, and regret. No person who contributed significantly to the world took the easy road. In what area have you been taking the easy road, and where could that road lead you? Magnify the consequences in your imagination until you can feel the outcome of neglect. Think of how much you can miss out on by taking the easy road. Think of the legacy that you will forfeit by taking the easy road. Think of how selfish you'd be if you only thought of your own comfort and how that might impact others. The easy road is for the crowd, and the crowd isn't going anywhere good. **You are not the crowd**.

13

FEEL Strong, PLAY Strong, BE Strong, LOOK Strong

"Never underestimate the power of getting up, dressing up, and showing up."

Ronnie Doss

After the pandemic in 2020, many people began working from home. In-office work was replaced with people sitting at their dining room tables on remote Zoom sessions alongside their coworkers. Not only did people begin to miss the camaraderie of working together in an office, they began to be casual with how they dressed. Over time, performance dropped in various professional fields, costing many companies large amounts of revenue. When we don't put ourselves in environments that force us to dress appropriately, we tend to perform in a subpar fashion. No, you don't have to dress in a suit and tie or a pantsuit, for that matter. However, there is something to be said about caring enough about your appearance that you will take a little extra time to dress nice. Remember, you only get one chance to make a first impression. Why should anyone take you seriously if you don't dress the part? How long has it been since you've updated your wardrobe? Dress up for a week, do your work, and see how your performance improves.

14

INSECURITY Is The Place Where STRENGTH Grows BEST

"Without understanding insecurity, you can never know the beauty of feeling confident. Confidence is developed when we consistently execute decisions that require courage."

Ronnie Doss

Focusing on your strengths is a great way to feel good about yourself, but working through fear and things that cause you to feel weak is the best way to grow stronger and feel better about yourself. What is a fear that you have that is holding you back? Where did that fear begin? How would your life be different if you were to face the fear, grow beyond it, and produce better things as a result? Everyone is afraid of something. Past hurts can cause us to be overly sensitive to certain situations. Our memories can often be suppressed, eventually producing underlying fear and doubt that causes us to avoid certain risks. I've heard it said, "A risk a day keeps mediocrity away." Fear can cause us to avoid making courageous choices and accept a mediocre life. Mediocrity begins with 'ME,' and if I want it to change, I must face my fears and move ahead. Yes, you may be scared, and yes, you may feel weak, but pushing forward will build your self-confidence and improve your output in every area. No matter where you go, there you are. You have to decide what version of you that you want to be there.

15

PRESSURE Breaks WEAK Things And Causes STRONG Things To BEND

"The struggle leads to stronger with every intentional step."

Ronnie Doss

When you look at a forest and see how high the trees have grown, they don't get to those heights because they are weak. We, like trees, grow when we have the strength and courage to bend when necessary. Pressure provokes old programs, and old programs can cause us to break when the pressure is high. A great example of enduring the storms and difficulties in life is the enormous trees in the Redwood Forest. The trees are able to grow so high because their root systems are overlapping. One tree's root system interlocks with another tree and then another. Together, they grow strong and tall, helping one another to endure the winds and storms. Having a support system around you to help you move past old paradigms and belief systems is one of the most important things you can have. When life's challenges hit you, your support system can help you bend versus break. We all have weaknesses in some areas, but that does not mean they must break us. If you're unwilling to bend because your old belief systems won't allow it, you will eventually break and lose everything you have worked for. Keep the goal, bend the approach, and watch yourself grow stronger. You and your goals are worth it.

16

CRY Your Way Into CLARITY

"Real men DO cry. It's okay to let it out. It's absolutely okay not to be okay sometimes."

Ronnie Doss

Mature individuals do cry; they just don't cry forever. Everyone with any emotional maturity will cry at some time or another. Being willing to feel emotion all the way through is one way to move yourself out of the bottom of the emotional barrel. What doesn't get expressed becomes suppressed, what is suppressed becomes depressed, and what is depressed can eventually become toxic. Being willing to cry and release your emotions is one way to clear the residue from your eyes. As a result, your vision for how to move forward can become clearer. If you have experienced a loss, allow yourself to feel it. Whether personal or professional, life is hard, and we all take the hits. Crying is a form of release that is good for your soul. Crying releases specific hormones and natural painkillers that can help to ease a person's discomfort. Individuals who don't allow themselves to feel pain eventually express the pain through some sort of health issue. The release is healthy. If you need to, watch a movie that brings certain emotions to life. Allow yourself to feel those emotions and talk to someone about them when they arise. When you talk about things that hurt you, you build empathy and trust with others and begin to heal the wounds that bring you pain. Add some motion to the emotion and commit to moving forward in a more clear and healthier way.

17

ANGER Needs A REASON And A TARGET

"Anger is often the most destructive emotion because it destroys you from the inside, and you don't even realize you're enjoying it."

Ronnie Doss

When you get angry, who receives the brunt of it? We tend to direct our anger at someone or something when things do not go our way. It is okay to be angry; it's natural, but staying angry or taking your anger out on someone else can be detrimental to your relationships. Anger can be a motivator for many people, but its presence in their day-to-day lives can ruin their peace of mind, mental health, and physical well-being. All anger is fueled by "rightness." The less you have to be right about something that elicits anger, the more you can retain your peace. When you are angry, do you ever question yourself as to why you are choosing anger? Have you ever considered that when you are angry, you are simply committed to being right more than you are committed to not ruining your day? Have you noticed that when you are angry, your focus is on your perspective and your feelings? Anger rarely cares about the solution; it is only concerned with expression. Is being right about your perspective worth disrupting your joy and your peace? Is your perspective more important than those who have to deal with your negative energy? Who typically takes the heat for it? Is there anyone you owe an apology to, including yourself, for how your "rightness" has sometimes turned to resentment? I challenge you to try not having to be right about things when they are disrupting your peace.

18

Feeling Like You Have To Be BUSY Is As MISERABLE As Doing All The Things You DON'T ENJOY

"When a person believes they must save the whole world, they miss the first opportunity to save themselves."

Ronnie Doss

To-do lists tend to be lengthy; success lists are short and concise. People who always believe they have to be doing something can never rest. Rest is an investment in your health. Doing things you do not love can be difficult, but constantly feeling like there is something more to do is torture. Rest fuels creativity, and busyness fuels bitterness and burnout. When a person recognizes that they are not the savior of the world and can allow their ego to rest, they begin to receive downloads of ideas that will produce stronger results with less wasted resources. Busy is a blessing only for a short while. Once you fall into the pattern of being busy all the time, you will never be able to enjoy all the things you were trying to be busy for. You do not always have to be busy, and people will still love you if you stop acting that way. Be productive, not just busy. How would your life change if you began to say "NO" more often? What is one thing you need to start saying "no" to that would free up much of your time and energy?

19

You Can't Protect Your Heart If You ALLOW YOURSELF To Continue ABUSING Your MIND

"You are always running a movie in your mind. You must decide whether that movie is compelling or torturous."

Ronnie Doss

What we hear time and time again eventually becomes our truth. Your truth is the filter that causes you to respond emotionally to the world you see. How you talk to yourself and allow others to speak to you will eventually impact your heart in many ways. Small conversations around and within you ultimately compound into a perceived truth that dictates what you look for and what you see. What you look for, you will always find. So, be careful what you tell yourself you should be looking for. Who or what are you allowing into your headspace that is causing you to be frustrated, insecure, or unmotivated? It may be time to make some changes all the way around. You may not be able to change who is around you, but you can change who is around you. Read that again!

20

BURNING BRIDGES Will Eventually Create A Smoke That Makes It IMPOSSIBLE To BREATHE

"The best way to get a breath of fresh air is when you have clean air and a clear conscience."

Ronnie Doss

Throughout our lives, there will be many people who frustrate and disappoint us. One of the tendencies we often feel is to respond with animosity and resentment. When we do or say things to hurt someone who has hurt us, it may feel suitable for a moment, but it only strengthens the power of negative energy that provoked us to begin with. Negativity becomes normal when we don't deal with it properly. With enough negative residue living within us, death gets on us and makes it impossible to live a healthy life. Connectivity is the key to a healthy existence, and that can't happen if you burn connections the moment they don't meet your preferences. What is one bridge you have burned in your life, and how would you handle the situation differently now?

21

SMALL ACHIEVEMENTS Only ACCUMULATE When They're Stacked On PURPOSE

"Purpose pulverizes procrastination."

Ronnie Doss

With so many distractions placed in front of us every day with advertisements and the mass media, it is easy to be compelled to do whatever is fastest and easiest. There are unlimited stories of people who have spent their lives climbing the ladder of success only to realize the ladder was not leaning on purpose. School doesn't give us purpose; careful consideration of our passions and talents gives us purpose. You may not have only one purpose, but many. There are many ways we can serve the world on purpose, and it is our responsibility to search to find out what those ways are. What good is it to win at someone else's game? If you are unsure what your purpose may be, get around people excited about their purpose and what they plan on doing with it. Inspiration is contagious and can push us toward discovery.

22

MOMENTS Are FLEETING; CAPTURE ONE or LOSE ONE

"Don't aspire to retire. Aspire to create beautiful memories you can take with you through eternity."

Ronnie Doss

It only takes being present for a moment to see all the wonderful things around us. It only takes a moment to miss all the beauty surrounding us. People who have children can tell you how quickly time flies when you're busy being a parent. One minute, your child begins to walk, and the next minute, they are walking across the stage at graduation. Moments can slip away if we don't open our eyes and hands to receive and experience them. Have you ever been so busy throughout your day that you forgot what you had for lunch? Have you ever been in such a hurry to drive somewhere that you didn't even realize music was playing on the radio? Slowing down to breathe and take inventory of your surroundings is one of the best ways to realize you are alive. If you aren't "now here," you are simply "nowhere." Make a memory with someone by engaging in a deeper conversation. Ask questions to the people you are with and listen to what they have to say. Proximity doesn't mean closeness; presentness does. Practice giving yourself to the present moment and pay attention to details you may have missed. Life comes to us in the details, and it will be up to us to recognize them.

23

When We Become Versed In ADVERSITY, We Learn To Speak The Language Of SOLUTION

"Losers look for excuses. Leaders look for problems and create ways to solve them."

Ronnie Doss

Without problems, there can be no need for solutions. Some people will say that problems are just opportunities disguised as challenges. All great leaders have had to overcome adversity in one way or another. The diamond was once a piece of coal that endured lots of pressure. The pearl is a result of an irritation inside the oyster. Creativity is often birthed out of adversity. Everyone has heard the phrase, "Easy come, easy go." If everything were easy, we would have no appreciation for value. Individuals who become valuable to the people around them are the ones who are looking for ways to face adversity and develop solutions. The takers in life are the ones who only want to make withdrawals from society and live off of the resources others create. We become resourceful when we recognize that the most valuable resources are typically found beneath the surface and that digging for solutions is the only way to uncover them. Adversity, though often unwelcome, possesses a profound beauty in its ability to shape and strengthen the human spirit. Much like a sculptor's chisel against marble, adversity has the power to reveal the inner beauty of resilience and fortitude that lives within each of us. Don't run from adversity; embrace it and step into your power.

24

EXCUSES Are WELL-THOUGHT-OUT DIRECTIONS Leading To The EASY WAY OUT

"Excuses always sound best to the person making them."

Ronnie Doss

You may like sharing your excuses, but no one wants to hear them. You even begin to believe it if you tell yourself an excuse long enough. Unforeseen events will happen, but that doesn't mean we should make it a habit of making excuses. The more excuses you make, the easier it is to make them and make them faster. We can rationalize any excuse with enough thought. Rationalize simply means "rational lies." The truth is, when we are committed to making something happen, we can make it happen. Suppose for some reason we can't deliver the promised outcome by the time we agreed to. In that case, we should simply renegotiate with the person or persons we made the agreement with, including yourself, and begin again with a stronger commitment. Our society seems to be run by people that are blaming others for poor outcomes. The "victim characters" place blame and create excuses to uphold their public image. Excuses are the work of a victim's mind, and the only way we can move past those excuses is to take absolute ownership of the results we produce. Results are the feedback of our daily choices. Results are the name of the game. Results reign supreme. How would your life be different if you spent the majority of your time executing your strategy rather than strategizing your excuses? Your actions speak so loud that people can't hear a word you say. It's time to own and execute your plan of attack.

25

PRESSURE Is A PRIVILEGE For Those COMMITTED To PRODUCTIVITY

"When you become grateful for the pressure, your productivity leads to the prize."

Ronnie Doss

No pressure, no prize. The people who respond positively to pressure are the ones who win. Great performers, athletes, entrepreneurs, and leaders all rise to the occasion when pressure presents itself. Pressure within the engine is what makes it powerful; handling the pressure presented to us in stressful situations is what makes us powerful. There is a reason it's called "under pressure": it feels like the weight of the world is on our shoulders when we are in a difficult situation. However, our ability to strengthen our core and retain our footing can help us lift ourselves above the pressure and see the solutions that lie above us. Pressure tends to push us down and try to keep us there. Our response to pressure by utilizing our gifts, exercising our talents, and rallying the resources we have around us is the only way to prevail. Pressure produces innovation when appropriately perceived. Pressure can inspire growth, instigate teamwork, and refine decision-making. Be proud that there is pressure and use it to propel you forward. Remember, the professionals love the pressure and perform. The amateurs despise the pressure and run. Which will you be?

26

You BEHAVE At Your LEVEL Of BELIEF

"Our behavior is as intertwined with our beliefs as our beliefs are intertwined with our feelings about life."

Ronnie Doss

Your confidence is like a muscle; you must make moves to keep it strong. Many people are not genuinely confident; they attempt to appear confident but are simply delusional because of their inexperience in a particular area. People often think they know something until they are placed in a situation where they need to exhibit their knowledge and be able to act accordingly with it. People who pretend to be wildly confident often overcompensate for something they feel they are lacking. People who exude no confidence at all are rarely willing to pursue anything worthwhile. When we strongly believe in our abilities due to practice, we are more likely to approach tasks with boldness, confidence, and resilience. Self-assuredness translates into proactive behaviors that lead to achieving more ambitious goals. Your attitude and actions will be determined by what you believe is possible. If you are serious about life, get serious about building your self-confidence. Start small and practice following through with simple action steps to build self-confidence. For example, think of exercising at the gym to build self-confidence; you can hurt yourself by trying to lift the heaviest weight. Start small, focus your energies, and quickly work your way up. Commitment, consistency, and courage are the catalysts for confidence. You've got what it takes. Make it happen!

27

EXPECTATIONS Must Only Be As HIGH As Your LEVEL Of CONTRIBUTION

"If you expect to keep getting invited to the table, you better be willing to bring something good to the table."

Ronnie Doss

Entitlement is where an individual believes that just because they are alive and breathing means they deserve good things in life. Nowhere is it written that anyone is owed anything in life. If we want something, we must be willing to get up and do the work necessary to receive compensation. Entitled individuals have unrealistic expectations of what they deserve, which leads to a lack of appreciation for the efforts of others. This mindset can breed resentment within an organization or family. Entitlement erodes. Entitlement irritates. Entitlement weakens. For an individual or team to create success, entitlement must be replaced with effort. Casualness must be replaced with cause, and complacency must be replaced with a commitment to the community. When everyone believes they deserve a trophy, the desire to work harder to win dissipates. Trophies must be earned, just like respect must be. I'll repeat it: *"No one owes you anything."* If you want it, earn it. We aren't children anymore; it's time to grow up and pay the price for what you say you deserve.

28

REBIRTH After You "KNOW IT ALL"

"The most valuable place in life is the place where you realize that all you have known means nothing."

Ronnie Doss

Possibilities die in the mind of an "expert." A true expert asks as many questions as they answer. You may think you know it all in one particular area, but there will always be more to uncover. Just when you think you know a person, something can uncover layers to them that you didn't know existed. Staying in pursuit of knowledge even after you think you know it all keeps your mind alive. People who retire often die soon after because they stop doing tasks that cause their brains to function on purpose. If we start to feel like we know it all, we lose the purpose to live. There is always a door on the other side of the door, and that door may lead to a horizon you never believed existed. Even the greatest minds of our time have admitted their own ignorance regarding the truths about life and our existence. If you fail to explore, you fail to exist. The expectation for more leads to exceptional experiences as we embark on the journey to arrive somewhere better. Expect more, experience more. You don't know, and that's a beautiful thing.

29

Talent Earns, But Wisdom KEEPS, MAINTAINS, And INCREASES

"Anyone can make a dollar, but only a wise person can turn what's earned into something more valuable."

Ronnie Doss

If you continually pour into a leaky vessel, it will always wind up empty. For wealth to remain in your life, wisdom must first enter your mind. My mother used to say, "The youth is wasted on the young." She meant that youthful energy given to young people isn't typically appreciated. When we learn to value resources such as health and vitality, we stop wasting those resources on things that don't matter. What difference does it make if you have a new car but don't feel like taking it out for a drive? What difference does it make if you have new clothes but don't feel like going anywhere special to wear them? What difference does it make how nice your home is if you are confined to one room? Earning money is really not that hard. The problem with our society is that we exchange our health for money and then spend the money trying to get our health back. Wisdom creates a healthy balance between work and home. Wisdom creates a healthy balance between striving and enjoying. Wisdom grows things, while immaturity exhausts things—wisdom deposits where foolishness continually makes withdrawals. Talent may win the game now and then, but ones character wins the championship time and time again. Who is someone you admire for their wisdom, and what area of your life could you model after them?

30

The Person We LEAVE BEHIND Eventually Leads The CHARGE TOWARD MUTINY

"Minimum wage employees can take down million dollar corporations when they are not handled with respect and consideration."

Ronnie Doss

Great teams and organizations understand that everyone on the team plays a vital role in its success. The janitor makes the environment clean so the surgeon can perform the operation. The person who takes the trash out is just as crucial to the function of the environment as the engineer who designed the waste system. All our roles overlap, even if we'd like to think that they don't. When we overlook people, they don't feel valued. People don't perform at their best when they don't feel valued. Reduced productivity leads to absenteeism and employee turnover. Over time, this can damage the organization's culture and reputation. When an organization's reputation is damaged, attracting and retaining top talent can make it more difficult. As a result, how we treat individuals at the bottom of the organizational chart will quickly impact how the people at the top can function. When people understand the importance of treating others how they want to be treated, a team can build better trust, collaboration, and morale. Without it, even the most talented teams eventually fall apart. Is there someone on your team or family that you have been overlooking? If so, what can you do to make the correction, starting now?

31

PRODUCTIVITY Is A Reflection Of PROMISES KEPT

"There are no small agreements.
They all matter."

Ronnie Doss

Productivity is a result of focused attention and effort. When we make promises to perform, we are vowing to make the effort and follow through till the completion of the agreement. Agreements make relationships stronger. When we keep our agreements, our relationship with ourselves grows stronger as well. When you know you can count on yourself to keep your word, you are more willing to step into opportunities that require the best of you. When you can't count on yourself, you will attempt only easy tasks and make no firm promises to perform. Over time, people will learn that they can't count on you in pressure situations and that you are not a strong team player. Your word is your bond, and if your word means nothing, your bond is useless. Relationships are built on agreements, so if you aren't willing to stick to your word, your relationships will be superficial and shallow. Weak people make weak agreements, and strong people make strong agreements. In Japanese samurai traditions, a samurai warrior would fall on his own sword before breaking his word. Honoring your word helps people trust you, believe in you, and be more willing to offer you more opportunities to excel. When you don't keep your word, you slowly stop believing in yourself. When you stop believing in yourself, the world stops believing in you. Would you trust yourself knowing how you keep your agreements? If not, what needs to shift in relation to how you see yourself so that you are more committed to keeping your word? Your words have the power to bring life or death to your situation. You can use your words to forge great bonds or erode your connections. Only you can give your word, and only you can keep your agreements. Choose your words wisely and use them well.

32

There Is POWER In The Word "NO"

"Goals may begin with a YES but are achieved and maintained with a willingness to say NO."

Ronnie Doss

You don't have to agree to things that deplete your soul. Saying "no" today creates more room for a "yes" later. YES is a powerful word. When you say YES, you open yourself up to a new experience. However, many of the experiences we commit to do not serve us well. When we set boundaries, we are willing to say NO to things that infringe on our peace and cause us to feel like we are acting out of obligation. Early in my career, I felt I should say YES to everything. I found myself traveling to places I didn't want to be and getting paid money that didn't feel like it was worth the exchange of energy it took to get there. Yes, we all have to pay our dues. Yes, we all need to do the work and earn a seat at the table. However, if the table you are sitting at doesn't serve health to your body and mind, you need to be willing to say NO to the seat and step away. Saying YES is a reaction to excitement. Saying NO is a response to respect. You must respect yourself enough to set boundaries, prioritize your time, and say NO to things that lead to the same ol' same ol'. You can't say YES to the mission if you keep saying YES to mediocrity.

33

INTELLECT Is Not A Result Of WHAT YOU READ But What You Are WILLING TO REREAD

"Time and repetition determine what we accept as deep truth."

Ronnie Doss

The words we hear make small impressions on our psyche that eventually mold our minds. The things that are whispered become screams if we hear them enough times. I had a mentor who would always say, "People need to hear things at least seven times before they stick." If you want knowledge, ideas, and principles to stick with you, you must make your mind sticky through repetition. Very few people have a photographic memory. The average human will forget a majority of the things they read and learn on a day-to-day basis. Repetition is the "mother" of all learning. When I speak at events, many people will tell me how many books they read and how long they read each day. I appreciate their excitement, but when I ask them to explain what they are learning from their reading, there isn't typically much they have to share. After a short period of time, reading can become a waste of time if we are not retaining what we see on the page. The lines become a blur, and we miss the context of the content if we aren't intentionally focused. Intelligent people do not simply read; they reread information again and again. A powerful tool to retain information is to write what you learn. Typing is good, but writing is much better. Keep a journal and number the insights that you write down. Go back to the journal repeatedly to reread what you have written. A journal of wisdom that you can reread time and time again is a great way to keep your mind sharp and robust knowledge on the tip of your tongue.

34

SUCCESS Doesn't Always FEEL Like SUCCESS

"The most successful people I know often feel like they are losing."

Ronnie Doss

Success is a long game. It requires constant uncertainty, continual pivots, emotional highs and lows, and a tolerance for stress. An often misconception about success is that it means living the "high life." People believe what they see on Instagram, TikTok, and Facebook, highlighting fancy cars, designer clothes, mansions, and expensive jewelry. Our society is being misled by "influencers" that motivate people by dangling pictures and video reels of luxury possessions in front of the viewers, showing off the liabilities many of the "successful" people have acquired. One thing is certain: anyone who has created real success will tell you it takes real work to make success happen. Many entrepreneurs share some of the dark times they had to go through on their way to the top of their industry. Long days and sleepless nights are common to those who have endured the process of becoming successful.

34

SUCCESS Doesn't Always FEEL Like SUCCESS

continued

As you read this book, you're probably thinking of changes you may need to make to your daily routine as you continue your journey toward a successful life. An improvement to your daily routine is only one part of the formula. Not only will you have to improve your daily routine to move forward more efficiently, but you will also have to improve how you think, how you speak, and who you associate with. You will have to be willing to sacrifice your time presently to gain something more desirable in the future. The emotional drain that can come from pursuing your goals is difficult. It is said that overnight successes usually take at least ten years to happen. Those ten years will be filled with disappointments, letdowns, setbacks, and anxiety. There will be times when you will wonder if you have what it takes to complete the tasks at hand. You will doubt yourself and others. You will cry, and you will lose sleep. It's part of the game. However, feelings are liars; just because you may not feel like you're moving forward doesn't mean you aren't. When you're in an airplane traveling 500 miles per hour, you may not realize how fast you are moving. Success is very similar. Set your path, face the resistance, and keep making adjustments to the flight plan. Whether you feel momentum or not, you will eventually arrive at your destination if you keep pushing ahead.

35

TRANSITION Always Feels Like FAILURE When You're RIGHT IN THE MIDDLE OF IT

"It's the place between where you once left and where you want to be that is the scariest."

Ronnie Doss

Some people call it "No man's land." It's the unfamiliar place we can find ourselves when we decide to leave something so familiar to us. Whether it be a job, city, or relationship that we are leaving, unfamiliar places can be extremely daunting. Like riding a roller coaster, stepping into the unknown can set us up for the ride of our lives. What sounds like screams of terror can become screams of excitement. Can you remember how nervous you were about starting elementary school? Can you remember how scared you were to leave your parents as they dropped you off on the first day? Think about how quickly your fear turned to joy and how excited you were to get to school and see your friends. With a bit of courage and time, what was once an imagination becomes a necessity. Dreaming for more can cause us to feel nervous and excited. Those feelings remind us we are alive and can make the journey as exciting as we want. Looking at the word transition, you see the letters SIT right in the middle. The tendency is to sit down and cover our heads during a transition. It's like a storm that we may try to keep ourselves safe from by sitting still. However, when we choose to STAND tall during the transition, we can see further ahead than we would have if we had chosen to sit still. When we can catch a glimpse of the horizon ahead of us, it can give us the necessary fuel to keep pressing forward even when the terrain is unfamiliar. All great explorers pushed through the transitions of leaving one place for the next. You and I were born to explore. Don't be afraid. Don't die before you are dead. Pick your destination and move with excitement and urgency. You will get there if you keep pressing toward the mark.

36

If You Live For APPLAUSE, You Will Die When It GETS QUIET

"Pray for people that want fame, and pray for those that have it."

Ronnie Doss

How many examples exist of individuals who achieved fame and destroyed their lives? Movie stars, rock stars, athletes, performers, and all others in between have sabotaged their lives by allowing fame to take them down the wrong path. Yes, everyone wants to be known, valued, and accepted, but applause is intoxicating. When an individual is desperate for the approval of others, they forget about developing their own self-acceptance. When the applause dies down, many people living off the adrenaline rush crash and burn. Alcohol, drugs, and unhealthy lifestyles become the norm for individuals who never learned the self-care necessary to transition back into a "normal" life. Yes, it seems sexy to have cameras flashing in your face because the world wants to see you, but how often do we see those people who were once in the limelight living in a dark, secluded place? Comedians, singers, musicians, and television stars often seem to be cursed with the things so many people think they want. Comedian Jim Carrey once said, "I wish everyone could be famous for a day so that they would know it is not all it's cracked up to be." Living a normal life, going into public, and not being hounded by the paparazzi and fans wanting a selfie is a beautiful and peaceful thing. Be grateful for where you are, and if you want to be famous, be famous in your own home amongst your spouse and children.

37

When You Have A GOAL, You Know The TARGET. When You're ACHIEVING GOALS, You BECOME A TARGET

"The higher you climb on the ladder of success, the larger the bull's eye on your back becomes."

Ronnie Doss

When you begin to make a name for yourself and become a public figure, people will inevitably come out of the woodwork. Aunts, uncles, cousins, schoolmates, or even people who met you in some random place will claim to be your best friend. People you never heard from while you were grinding your way to the top will suddenly appear on your radar, not always with the best intentions. People may want money from you, they may want you to make connections for them, or maybe they want to tell them the secrets that got you to where you are. Either way, success can make you a target. Keeping your personal reputation, as well as your professional reputation intact, is important. None of us are perfect, but we can surely thwart the arrows of those who may want to take us down by keeping our house in order. I have heard countless stories of athletes who came into lots of money when they became professionals, only to lose it because people around them were using them or even mismanaging funds for them. There is a quote that says, "When you have money, your friends know you; when you have no money, you will know your friends." Success attracts people and opportunities, but it doesn't always mean those people or opportunities are best for you. As you continue to create more success and have access to the resources that come with it, assess and take inventory of who is around you and what their true motives might be. Would those same people be there if you couldn't provide them with some sort of handout? Would those people still be in your corner supporting and encouraging you if you were at the bottom of the ladder? People who are genuinely for you are for you regardless of whether you are winning or losing. People who only want to associate with you because you have something that can make their lives easier are not truly your friends. They don't love you. They love what you can provide for them. There's a big difference; the sooner you realize that, the less weight you'll have to carry to the top.

38

Take Your RIGHTFUL PLACE or One Will Be PROVIDED For YOU

"If you allow someone else to decide your destiny, it will always be less than what it could have been, and you'll end up resenting yourself and them for putting you there."

Ronnie Doss

Taking your rightful place as it pertains to your goals and dreams is crucial for fulfillment. It involves recognizing that you have the power to shape your life through your choices and attitude. When you embrace ownership, you move helplessness and victim-mindedness behind you. When you take responsibility for your destiny, you acknowledge that your circumstances, although influenced by external factors, are ultimately shaped by your focus, your responses, and the energy you direct toward the desired outcomes. When you take ownership of your future, you make wiser decisions more consistently because you weigh those decisions against the positive outcome you could create. Without ownership, all decisions are permissible, and the consequences mean nothing. Ownership breeds responsibility, and responsibility strives for accountability. By taking ownership of your destiny, you become the architect of your future versus being a victim of it. Either own your destiny, or you'll always be at the mercy of those committed to fulfilling theirs. Which will you choose?

39

STABILITY Releases ABILITY

"It's difficult to be creative when your mind is exhausted from trying to survive in an unfamiliar place."

Ronnie Doss

Finding a safe place where your mind can relax paves the way for enhanced creativity. When your mind is calm and free from stress, you are more open to new ideas and unconventional thinking. In this state, the brain is less inhibited by rigid thought patterns and more receptive to unique connections between different concepts. The mental freedom that comes from a place of stability allows us to explore various possibilities without the constraints of self-doubt or fear of failure. A stable place can foster fertile ground for creativity to flourish. When we find a place where we can settle in and relax a bit, cortisol levels begin to fall, which in turn reduces anxiety and mental tension. As a result, we can better focus on the task at hand and engage in deep, uninterrupted contemplation. The heightened focus and clarity of mind enables us to get into more of a creative flow, which leads to the generation of imaginative ideas. Stability allows us to thrive where uncertain ground causes us to merely survive. In essence, it can be extremely beneficial for us to stick with a job long enough to feel stability and create some innovation. Bored is not necessarily bad if we use boredom to allow our minds to see new visions and dream new dreams. Give it time before you rush to the next thing. There could be acres of diamonds right under your feet.

40

There Will Always Be Wounds From The BATTLES YOU REFUSE TO FIGHT

"The battle for the life you desire must be fought and won. If you won't pick up your weapon and conquer the enemy that stands between you and your dreams, the wound of regret will grow deeper until it eventually infects your soul."

Ronnie Doss

There are two versions of you. There is a version of you that faces your fears, confronts your beliefs, and takes action even when you doubt yourself. The other version is the one that cowers down in the presence of uncertainty. This version always looks for shortcuts and easy roads. Every day, you get to choose which version you will be. The assertive version that is focused and determined will take on new challenges and rise to the occasion. The lesser version will try and fly below the radar, making itself invisible to threats. The lesser version produces mediocre results and manifests a frustrated and resentful spirit. The lesser version will never know the thrill of setting a big goal and crushing it. The lesser version will never know how it feels to scale the mountain and see a view only the disciplined can experience. The assertive version asks for opportunities and, when there are none, creates some. Children who have been pampered their whole lives grow into adults with no tough skin or resilience. Our society is breeding people who want something for nothing. A war must be engaged for an individual to achieve great things and pave the way for legacy. The war is with oneself, one's perception, and a continuous battle to defeat the need for comfort and ease. If you want to be victorious, you must be willing to fight for something. If you don't fight, you'll lose all that could be yours.

41
BEAUTIFUL LOSERS

"Some people have a beautiful smile and a filthy spirit. Looks can be deceiving."

Ronnie Doss

Have you ever seen a beautiful landscape, such as a glacier or volcano? Even though they are attractive and enticing to the eye, they can be dangerous and even deadly to the rest of you. People are no different; just like beautiful icicles hanging from a ledge or an electrical storm lighting up the sky, these stunning spectacles to look at can do so much damage in just a moment. The icicle falls and hurts or kills someone below, or the lighting strikes, electrocuting some unlucky victim. Many things in life may be easy on the eyes but terrible for our peace of mind. Some of the most attractive people I have ever met have been the most insecure and superficial. It only takes one or two encounters with someone who appears beautiful to see beyond their skin and into their being.

41

BEAUTIFUL LOSERS

continued

Maya Angelou said, "When someone shows you who they are, believe them." This is not to say that we all don't slip up and behave in ways that we may not be proud of, but just because someone looks like a person that you might want to be around, remember, beauty is only skin deep, but nasty can go all the way to the bone. Individuals who rely solely on their looks to get their way are what I call 'beautiful losers.' These individuals will use their looks, along with some good social media filters, to gain viewers' attention and then spew their toxic messages to those who will listen. Beautiful losers are posers, pretenders, and backstabbers who cover themselves with makeup to appear perfect in every way. Beneath the surface, though, these people are not. They can be self-centered and narcissistic and only concerned with how they look and never consider how they may cause others to feel. A scripture in the Bible says, "You shall know them by their fruit." The passage references how people can be judged by what they produce in their lives, not by how they look. You can put lipstick on a pig, but that doesn't change what the pig is. Pay attention; you will see much more than what is on the surface.

42

Not EVERYTHING Has To Be EXCITING!

"If everything has to be exciting, you'll end up empty and exhausted."

Ronnie Doss

Our society thrives off of entertainment and fun. We buy things because we believe they will make our lives more convenient and enjoyable. We have pushed the limits of convenience to the point that almost everything has to be easy and fun. Over the years, I have found that the healthiest things we can do are often the most boring. When we do things in private that strengthen our abilities, we can perform in public with excellence. Practice never looks perfect, and it doesn't necessarily feel that way, either. When we do things that aren't exciting, we create a life where we experience exciting things that others may not get to. When we get up early, eat properly, and push our bodies with exercise, it may not feel exciting at the time, but it is necessary for a healthy and exciting future. When you are healthy, you have the strength to create exciting things; when you are not healthy, things just aren't exciting overall. Even though doing one more rep of exercise, drinking one more ounce of water, or reading one more chapter of a book may not be exciting, it is making way for more exciting things to come your way. Don't overlook the beauty of the boring stuff because boring is often the soil from which exciting things grow.

43

Playing The VICTIM CHARACTER Will Have It's Benefits But Is NEVER WORTH THE COST

"Every choice we make has costs and benefits."

Ronnie Doss

I've done it, and so have you! There have been times when you've allowed an excuse, a story, or a circumstance to provoke you into playing a character that tells you you are out of control. What I call the "Victim Character" is when we think, talk, and behave like the world is doing something terrible to us. Or that our past has done something to us that we will never be able to move forward from. As I just mentioned, there are benefits to choosing the victim character. You no longer have to be accountable when playing the victim character. The thing causing you to play the victim is now in control. The ex-spouse, ex-boss, current employer, neighbor, co-worker, kid, or family member is now the reason you don't have control of your emotions, and you're okay telling yourself that story. In life, you will be a victim from time to time. You can be a victim of abuse, neglect, theft, gossip, or backstabbing. However, just because you were victimized doesn't mean you are a victim.

43

Playing The VICTIM CHARACTER Will Have It's Benefits But Is NEVER WORTH THE COST

continued

You do not have to play the victim to how you were raised, your parents, your education, your financial status, or what part of town you live in. The benefit of playing the victim is that you are off the hook regarding accountability and responsibility. Still, it will cost you all the good things you could have created if you had chosen the alternative character. The alternative to the victim character is what I call the responsible character. While the victim says, "Life is being done to me, and I am out of control," the responsible character says, "I am at cause for my experience at any given time." So, even if someone victimized me, I don't have to allow that to control my emotions. By taking responsibility for where I put my focus, I can control my emotions much better. When a person takes responsibility for their experience at any moment, they can ask themselves why they chose that experience. Yes, there will be natural tendencies to respond to trauma and loss, but we do have the ability to decide how long we stay with the experience. We can choose to remain there permanently, or we can choose to take responsibility for our focus and thinking and then take steps to leave the negative situation behind. People playing the victim character always blame someone or something, even if they don't admit it. A person's energy can strongly indicate whether they are stuck in the victim character or choosing to be responsible. Responsibility eventually leads to better results and stronger self-confidence.

44

What's Your FAVORITE "FAILURE"?

"You are going to fall short, and you're going to fail. Take the lessons you learn, leave the shame, and keep moving forward toward your next level."

Ronnie Doss

What failure have you learned the most from? Whether it's a lost opportunity, failing the test, losing a job, missing a promotion, or ruining a relationship, what is something that you have gone through that has taught you the most valuable lessons? It takes time to appreciate what you have, including the wisdom due to some failure. I am not saying you should ever sabotage an opportunity to see what else might be ahead for you, but I am saying that failure shouldn't cause you to quit. I've heard many people say, "Fail fast, fail often, fail forward." The point is that failure offers many great opportunities for us to begin again with more insight than we had before. Walt Disney was fired from a newspaper for "lacking creativity" several years before he created such iconic characters as Mickey Mouse and started the Walt Disney Company. Oprah Winfrey overcame an impoverished upbringing to become one of the most influential media personalities in the world. She began in poverty and has since become a billionaire businesswoman. She made mistakes along the way but didn't let them stop her from doing the work that took her to incredible heights. Steve Jobs, co-founder of Apple Inc., was fired from the company in the mid-1980s. Jobs continued developing innovative ideas and eventually returned to Apple, where he played a crucial role in revitalizing the company and overseeing the development of the iPod, iPhone, and iPad. All the individuals just mentioned dealt with failure. If these individuals experienced failure and came back stronger, what could you do if you began to see your failures as lessons and motivators instead of punishments and errors? It may also be wise to ask yourself whose mistakes you are currently learning from. Wise people study other people's mistakes and learn from them also. Maybe you could make it a point to move forward from here, looking for lessons in everything, even your favorite failure.

45

UNIVERSAL PRINCIPLES Will Always Reward Your SPECIFICITY

"Without knowing the goal, you can run up and down the field all day long and never know if you actually score."

Ronnie Doss

A lack of clarity on direction can be one of the most confusing and frustrating things an individual or team can experience. It's difficult to get people on the same page if you don't even know what the page is. Clear direction is essential for organizations and individuals. When people can't measure their progress, they criticize their activity through the lens of assumption. However, assumption is the fastest way to be blindsided by truth. Procrastination becomes acceptable and normal when we are not clear on where we are going. With a lack of clarity, there is no sense of urgency because hurrying to be more lost is simply a waste of energy. Without clarity, we are lost a majority of the time. Imagine that you never get specific on the type of person you want to be in a relationship with and, as a result, never set any standards for yourself. As a result, everyone you meet becomes an option for you. The thief, the abuser, the molester, the addict, the flake, and the beautiful loser all become people to whom you give your focus. How do you think those relationships are going to work out? Do you think they are going to serve you well? Do you think they will inspire you to become great, or will they manipulate you into settling for mediocre things like them? The moment you choose to identify what you want and what you are willing to tolerate, the universe becomes your ally versus your enemy. Remember, more is not better; better is better.

46

HIGH STANDARDS Protect You From LOW-STANDARD EXPERIENCES

"Standards are a weapon that, when raised, can defeat the army of mediocrity and inadequacy."

Ronnie Doss

Standards are the tides that have the ability to raise all the ships. Relationships, partnerships, friendship, mentorship, and any other type of ship you can think of can rise when the standards in place demand it. People don't demand higher standards for themselves because they've never been exposed to scenarios where innovation and excellence have occurred. Social, cultural, and environmental factors can shape a person's mindset, limiting their belief in themselves and what they can achieve. When someone lacks confidence, they are more prone to accept what is given to them versus striving for more. Individuals may also lower their standards due to a fear of failure. The rationale a person may develop if they lack self-confidence is that if they do not attempt to achieve more, then they cannot fail and disappoint themselves or others. Regardless of a person's standards, the results they achieve and their demands on the world around them will reflect. It's easy to pass judgment on others based on what they have or the situations they allow themselves to be in, so it's better not to compare yourself to them. The purpose of standards is to help us produce more efficient and effective results for a world that desperately needs high-standard examples. High standards lead to higher quality options, which can help us enjoy the gift of life. It is tough to soar like an eagle when you have the standards of a chicken. Do yourself a favor and set higher standards for yourself. Don't accept the first thing that comes your way. Recognize your worth, and by displaying high standards, people will treat you accordingly. Never forget that you are always teaching people how they can treat you.

47

CONSIDER The FUTURE While Being PRESENT TODAY

"What will you do with all the time you save by hurrying everywhere?"

Ronnie Doss

The beauty of presentness is found in the moment. At a time when busyness is celebrated, embracing the moment and savoring the time we have is often dismissed as being casual or unassertive. However, when we immerse ourselves in the here and now, we can feel the bliss that comes when the sun shines upon our face or when the wind softly blows through our hair. We notice the flavors of a home-cooked meal and the abundance of sensory delights that are often overlooked and underappreciated. The beauty of presentness is that it reminds us of the profound simplicity of living fully in the moment. When we wholeheartedly engage in the present moment, we let go of the weight of worry and recognize that all we need in the present moment is already there. Embracing the moment enables us to let go of what was and what may come, granting us the freedom to inhabit the here and now fully. What good is the now if we miss it? Right now, right where you are, look around and notice something you haven't noticed before. Slow your breathing and allow yourself to be with the newly discovered thing by momentarily giving it your full attention. By doing this, you are practicing mindfulness, a magnificent way to feel more of the beauty life offers.

48

IGNORANCE Is Not BLISS And NEVER WILL BE

"What you continually turn a blind eye to eventually becomes a blind spot, and blind spots are where most accidents happen."

Ronnie Doss

Ignorance is often seen as a blissful state. This idea suggests that being uninformed leads to a happier, more carefree existence. However, this notion must be corrected, as it is inherently flawed. In reality, ignorance often leads to a plethora of negative consequences. Pretending not to know can lead to the same negative consequences as not knowing. Ignorance is not bliss, and pretending to be ignorant about something will not create bliss either. Essentially, ignorance will not create bliss; ignorance will create lack, poverty, sickness, and distress. Many people "play dumb" to uncover new answers, but others "play dumb" because they don't want to face the answers they already know. Continuing to do the same thing repeatedly and expecting the outcome to improve is an example of ignorance. Pretending not to know there are consequences to negative behavior is also ignorance.

Neglecting to do things that you know you need to do is ignorance. I have said it before: we do not need to know everything, but we must use the information we have to make better choices for our future. If not, we are no better off than someone with no information. Information is power when it is applied to action. The phrase goes, "Ready, aim, fire." It does not go, "Ready, aim, ignore." Maybe it's time to fire on the things that you've been pretending not to know. It could drastically change your life for the better.

49

UPGRADING WISDOM Means DOWNGRADING FEAR

"A wise question can cut straight to the heart of fear and shed light on the path that leads to courage"

Ronnie Doss

Fear runs rampant in our society due to rapid change and uncertainty in so many areas. Fear increases with each passing day. Political unrest, wars, cultural discord, and a volatile economy all contribute to the growing fears and concerns of the human race. Typically, when we address fear, we mention words like "boldness" and "courage" as the anecdote. Here, I would like to use the word WISDOM to counter fear and worry. Wisdom can offer us the insight and tools to navigate life's challenges in a healthy way. By gaining and applying wisdom, we can confront fear and move ahead more calmly with purpose. Fear is a primal emotion that has helped our civilization survive. It is a protective mechanism that alerts us to potential danger. Over time, though, fear has manifested as anxiety and insecurity regarding our abilities to function well in the future. This is where wisdom becomes effective. Wisdom can offer us an elevated perspective and enable us to see the challenges ahead for what they are. Challenges are simply opportunities. When I have wisdom or possess the ability to gain wisdom in a particular area, it undoubtedly helps me to avoid mishaps and missteps. Wisdom is a light to the path of progress. Take a moment and think of a few people that you would consider wise and formulate a list of questions to draw valuable insights from them. When we are willing to humble ourselves and ask questions, we can inevitably avoid many potholes that might have caused us harm. Create the list and start asking questions. You'd be amazed at the wisdom you have close at hand. Don't waste it.

50

If You're UNMOTIVATED, It's Because You're Being SELFISH!

"If all you focus on is you and how you feel, when you feel bad, the whole world seems bad too."

Ronnie Doss

One of my mentors used to say, "If you wake up in the morning and you're feeling unmotivated, it's because you're being selfish." He meant that if you don't feel motivated to do things, it's because you're not focusing on all the good there is to do for others. Being unmotivated indicates you are only concerned with your feelings, convenience, and comfort. I was taught that learning how to act your way into feelings is much more important than waiting to feel something before you act. Leaders create emotion with motion; mediocre people wait until the emotion is present before taking any action toward better. If you don't feel motivated, make an upbeat music playlist, turn on some inspirational videos on YouTube, or flip on an inspiring movie to get your brain firing off chemicals that can put you into a peak state. All sorts of external catalysts can help you to get moving and build momentum. Another powerful source of motivation can be an accountability partner. When you have a person that you must answer to for your actions, you will be much more prone to take action. Feeling unmotivated sometimes is normal, but we must not allow ourselves to stay there for long. There is so much life we can live and many people we can serve when we learn to become self-starters.

51

PRIZE Is On The Other Side Of PRICE

"Everyone wants the prize, but few are willing to pay the price that leads to it."

Ronnie Doss

I get up each day and work out. I tend to be at the office early and, many times, will stay late. I don't expect life to give me the prize of success if I am unwilling to do the work necessary to win it. We have become a society that believes that ALL things should be able to come to us quickly. I often speak of the "Amazon Prime" principle to groups I work with. To have something delivered to your doorstep fast, all you have to do is go to the Amazon App and order what you want. Many items can be delivered to you the next day, and in some cities, they can be delivered to you within just a few hours. Though this is wonderful for household items, success doesn't work like this. You have to go to the GET WORK DONE app and hit that button day in and day out to receive anything good. You can't purchase your way into success, and you can't post your way into significance. The only way to create success and feel like what you are doing is significant is to get up and get moving. Jack Dempsey said, "Champions get up even when they think they can't." You are going to have to decide if you want to be a champion or the person who gets beat to death by life. Maybe you are okay with being the best of the worst, but that's not what being a champion is about. Being your best means pushing yourself beyond the tendency to procrastinate, taking shortcuts, and giving only a half-hearted effort. If you want the prize, you must commit to the work that will provide it. Without the commitment, you'll produce nothing more than anyone else. Maybe that's okay with you, but I doubt it if you're reading this book!

52

PASSION Is The PERSUADER

"Passion is the energy that a purposeful life feeds off of."

Ronnie Doss

When you start to do things in alignment with purpose, you begin to burn bright with a passion that no one can take from you. A passion for something can overpower feelings of casualness, complacency, and a lack of self-discipline. Many people say that getting up and grinding is the secret to success, but I believe success comes down to two things: Passion and Persistence. Instead of simply going through the day without purpose, stop and ask yourself some questions to help you identify your purpose. What motivates you? Who inspires you? When have you felt most alive? Who can you help today? Asking yourself a few simple questions daily can align you with purpose, motivate you, and compel you to take massive action toward a more fulfilling life.

53

If You're Not Bringing Your A-GAME, It's Time To Find ANOTHER JOB

"If you aren't willing to bring your A-game to the team, it may be time for you to execute plan B and step off."

Ronnie Doss

I have heard it said, "You can't grow from what other people eat." People often join a new team, thinking that the team will make them a winner. That is not the way winning works. To be on a winning team, you must become a winner. No one likes working with a taker. No one likes being around a freeloader. While I am at it, I'll also say that no one wants to be around stingy, selfish, poverty-minded individuals either. The friends I surround myself with help me to think bigger and motivate me to play bigger. I have to make the final choice to take action, though. No one can make the final decision for me, and no one can do that for you. My friends have created great options for themselves and have many valuable possessions. I drive a Tesla Plaid. It's one of the fastest cars in the world and is quite expensive. This past weekend, someone said, "That car costs more than some people's house." Regardless of the price, I let my friends drive my car. I want them to experience it and enjoy it the way I have. I have friends who own beach houses and mountain cabins that continually offer me and my family time to stay there at no cost. You see, people who bring their A-game earn the respect of others. When people see you working hard to help out, they will be willing to do nice things to contribute to your life. Success leaves clues, and so does laziness. I have no problem helping people who are willing to help themselves. Are you giving your best, or are you just trying to get by with the least possible effort? Be honest. People are watching. If you are not already, now is a great time to start bringing your A-game!

54
Pigs Have No Idea That They STINK

"If you lay with dogs,
you'll eventually get fleas."

Ronnie Doss

Environment is seductive and so are "friend" groups. In the corporate world, the term RESPONSIBILITY CREEP is often used to describe how people gradually find themselves with more responsibilities because they never learned to say no. In our personal lives, the term IRRESPONSIBILITY CREEP can be just as real. Irresponsibility creep is where you become increasingly irresponsible because you have never learned to say no to negative people and their destructive behaviors. Those negative behaviors can slowly creep into your life as well. Have you ever walked into someone's home and noticed that it has a particular smell? Some people's homes may smell like candles, soaps, or even moth balls. Either way, the people living in the house don't even notice it anymore because their brains have gotten used to it. The more you are around people who gossip, the more gossip becomes your norm. The more you're around negative people, the more that negativity will be the norm for you. Your mind continually adapts to the things around you, so you better be cautious of what you give proximity to. If you're unsure how your attitude and energy may look to others, ask someone you trust to share open and honest feedback and make adjustments where you feel necessary. You wouldn't want negative attributes to become like the smells I mentioned before that are so easy to get accustomed to.

55

You Can't Fight TOMORROW'S BATTLES With YESTERDAY'S INFORMATION

"There is a huge difference between growth and delayed obsolescence."

Ronnie Doss

It is much easier to keep rehashing old information because it is what's normal to us. Information and the feelings we attach to that information can become so embedded in our psyche that we are scared to let the old knowledge die. Innovation is a key to being relevant in our world. Great companies that once dominated their industry faded away because they refused to change. Start-up companies offering new tools and resources to fit our ever-changing world are growing at incredible rates. If you think of yourself as a corporation, are the things you are learning and applying setting you up to be relevant in the future, or are you slowly becoming obsolete? Failure typically happens gradually and then suddenly. If you are not willing to take some risks and change your approach before it's too late, you may not be a competitor in the future game. If you believe you haven't come this far to stop, then you probably need to bring in some fresh new ideas and see what market share you can start to reach. Don't fall in love with what you know so much that you are blind to new possibilities. The future is bright; don't let what you think you already know blind you to it.

56

What You ELEVATE And CELEBRATE Displays What MEANS MOST TO YOU

"Who and what you are willing to lift up will eventually lift you."

Ronnie Doss

My wife and children are a driving force to my work ethic. I love providing them with fun resources and fun opportunities that cause them to feel excited about life. One of the greatest compliments I often hear is, "I love how you honor and celebrate your wife and children." I tell people that you can always tell how someone is doing by the size of the smile on their spouse's face. When you decide to get married, you are essentially committing to guarding and protecting your spouse at all costs. It becomes your job to guard and protect them from the negativity and drama that seems to be all around. If you aren't willing to protect your spouse emotionally and mentally, do you really love them? If you aren't honoring your family, do you really love them? Or are you just using them to help you build some personal agenda? No, I'm not saying to treat your spouse and children like they are helpless, but I am saying to make an effort to protect them from some of the stupidity that is so prevalent in our world. Don't allow craziness and immaturity to take its place at the dinner table. Set clear boundaries to protect your family from emotional abuse and manipulation. Stand guard at the gate of your home, protect the heart and mind of those closest to you by offering them wisdom and insight while also being their greatest encourager. You'd be amazed at what people can become when their hearts and minds are clear, and they know they have someone in their corner rooting them on.

57

The WORLD Still Needs HEROES

"You don't have to save the whole world,
but you can help save someone's day."

Ronnie Doss

When you see someone in need on the street and avoid them, it could be because you haven't considered what they need from you. We often think we have to solve the whole problem for someone when, in fact, we may just need to help them solve the problem that is right in front of them. Offering someone a few dollars for a warm meal or giving them a bottle of water doesn't solve all their problems, but it does solve a problem. When you help someone solve a problem, you are a hero in the moment. Heroes don't have to wear capes; they simply display compassion and empathy as their superpower. You and I both have superpowers, and we can all make a difference for someone. One of the most interesting things about helping others is how great it makes us feel. When we serve well, we feel well. If you're feeling down, do something nice for someone else and notice how it lifts your spirit. I once heard a wise man say, "Kindness is the only thing we can give away that never runs out." It may be time to step into your power and share your compassion with a world that desperately needs it. Opportunity is everywhere.

58

PROCRASTINATION Is PROTECTION From Something You've Attached A NEGATIVE FEELING TO

"We don't tend to procrastinate on the things we make ourselves excited about."

Ronnie Doss

When we procrastinate, it is typically because we have concluded that what we need to do will cause us some suffering. Because procrastination is such a well-known thing, I don't believe there is much need to describe it. What I will do is offer a quick solution. To break out of procrastination:

1. Magnify the consequences of what could happen if you do not take action.
2. Visualize the very worst-case scenario, make it as vivid as possible, feel it, and from that place, think of all the impact the worst-case scenario could have on you, your family, your career, and your overall well-being. Once you have allowed yourself to go to that dark place, the next step is to pull yourself out of it with a small action step.
3. Magnify a reward you will give yourself once you complete the task you have been putting off.
4. Do something really nice for yourself. Something that rewards you for pushing past hesitation.

We humans typically take action to gain pleasure or avoid pain. When you use both as catalysts for action, procrastination will have less of a hold on you. Moving beyond procrastination is a mind game. To succeed, you must be willing to play with intentionality.

59

DELUSION Is BELIEVING You Must Be MOTIVATED To ACT

"You don't have to feel good to do good."

Ronnie Doss

What you eat, how you sleep, what you've seen on TV, or even what you've read can determine how you feel on any given day. Motivation is a very circumstantial thing. You can be motivated, but the motivation disappears when the circumstances around you change. If you only go to work when you feel like it, you'll never get anything done. If you only exercise when you feel good, you'll never be in shape. If you are only kind to people when you feel like being kind, your relationships will suffer. Feelings are the most overrated thing when it comes to productivity. Feelings come and go, but commitment to action trumps it all. If I am truly committed to something, I can feel tired, have a headache, not be motivated, or even be in a bad mood. However, knowing that what I am committed to must be done at all costs, regardless of what my feelings may be saying to me, is a great way to strengthen my fortitude and get after it.

Pro athletes don't train just when they feel like it. Pros do the work regardless of how they feel. Professional writers don't just write when they feel like it; they make themselves sit down and put the pen to paper. Professional singers don't just go into the studio when they feel like it; they put themselves in the studio to see what they can create. If you only take action when you feel like it, you'll probably not be doing much the majority of the time. Fall in love with doing the work, and the results will come. Also, the more you love the work, the more the motivation to do it will present itself.

60
MESSES Create STRESSES

"It's hard to have inner calm when everything around you is in disorder. If you want to clear your mind, start with something as simple as organizing your sock drawer."

Ronnie Doss

Professional tennis player Andre Agassi once said, "If there is disorder in my tennis bag, there is disorder in my game." Andre was known for being meticulous about what could potentially affect his game. For him, it was everything. Clutter conflicts with clarity, and clarity is a must for high achievement. I was facilitating a corporate training recently, and one of the participants I was working with asked me if I had OCD (Obsessive Compulsive Disorder). I asked her why she would think that? She said, "Everything around your place at the conference table is in order. You seem to keep things aligned with one another and always return them to the same spot." She was right. My iPad lines up with the edge of the table. My phone sits in a straight line on top of the iPad. My pen is always placed horizontally in front of me, and anything else I may be using during my presentation has a place that "balances" my area out. I set up my presentation rooms accordingly as well. I like to keep things balanced and in order. When my mind is racing, I can slow it down by organizing my workspace. Rarely does my need for things to be in the right spot keep me from doing what needs to be done, but I must admit that I tend not to work as well when things around me seem out of place. The next time you feel like you can't get your thoughts in order, put your workspace in order. Start with your desk, straighten your pictures, and wipe the fingerprints off your screens. See if those simple steps might help you fire off good chemicals in your brain to help you get more focused and in a creative flow.

61

You Must Create A
DISTRACTION-FREE ENVIRONMENT

"Distraction leads to inaction, and inaction is not an option when you're playing at a high level."

Ronnie Doss

As I write this, I am in my office; it is quiet, and there are no distractions around me. My phone alerts are silenced, and no TV or music is playing in the background. It's just me and my Mac Book Pro. Finding a quiet place is a relatively simple thing to do. If you don't have a quiet place in your home, go to the library. If you can't go to the library, get some noise-canceling headphones and go to a closet. It's incredible how much you can accomplish with just a little quiet time. Many people say they never have any quiet time because they have children. My response is always, "Wake up before the distractions do." If you recognize that you need some quiet time or uninterrupted thinking time, you must make an effort to find or create that space. The world is busy, but that doesn't mean your mind must always be busy. Nikola Tesla said, "A busy mind and a disciplined mind are NOT the same." To discipline your mind, you must practice keeping your mind focused on the task ahead of you, and that's extremely hard to do when people are pulling at you. You need some non-negotiable YOU time, often requiring someplace to be alone. I don't write well when things are drawing my attention away. I can do it, but it's definitely not the best version of the thoughts I am trying to share. If you create a distraction-free environment and hold yourself accountable to being in that space focused on your work, I can assure you your personal productivity will increase substantially.

62

You Can Fake A Lot With 95 PERCENT COMMITMENT, But The FIVE PERCENT Can RUIN YOUR FUTURE

"I don't recommend telling your spouse you are 95 percent committed to your marriage! Your marriage, your children, your career, they all deserve the best of you."

Ronnie Doss

The commitment to get you to the door and the commitment that will move you through the door are not the same. Some people love to play the 99-yard dash game. They run like crazy toward the goal line, then sabotage themselves right before crossing it. Whether a person deals with insecurity, unworthiness, or feelings of inadequacy, being wholly committed to an endeavor is the only way to overpower those feelings and eventually win. Some talented people can give only half the effort and still outperform many others, but the person who does that knows truthfully they are not giving their best. You might be able to fool other people sometimes, but you can't fool yourself. Commitment is a personal thing! What do you see when you look in the mirror? Do you see someone you respect or someone you know is trying to sneak their way through life, only giving their best a small portion of the time? This is not to make you feel bad; this is about recognizing that you have much more to offer. When you do, you'll feel better and make a bigger difference for the people that matter most to you. It all starts with commitment.

63

**HARD WORK PUMPS GREATNESS
From Your Heart To The Rest
Of Your Extremities**

"Nothing waters the seeds of success like blood, sweat, and tears."

Ronnie Doss

You may be the strongest weight lifter in the world, but if your heart is weak, you won't have the stamina to lift for very long. Great fighters not only pack a strong punch but also have the cardiovascular strength to endure the many rounds of the fight. Courage, boldness, and commitment are all issues of the heart. Think of your life as a marathon. Are you doing the work to prepare yourself for the long race ahead? Are you conditioning your mind, body, and spirit to overcome some of the challenges that can manifest as you get older? Individuals who persevere are individuals who have hearts. If you think that your good looks and your family's money are going to be the things that make your life easy, you're wrong. All the good looks and money in the world can't insulate you from the truth about life. Life will beat you to your knees and leave you there to die. When life hits you, it's your heart that will push you to get back up. How's your heart? Are you training your heart to be strong in a cardiovascular sense? Are you training your heart in a figurative sense? To create long-lasting success, you will have to have both. Strengthen and guard your heart, for out of it flows the issues of life.

64

GOOD RESOURCES Aren't Drawn To People Who Remain In A BAD HEAD SPACE

"Poor is a state of mind; broke is a state of wallet."

Ronnie Doss

I have never once told my kids that we can't afford something. Never! We may not have budgeted for a particular purchase, but I will never say we can't afford something. Some people say things like, "Money doesn't matter to me." When they say that, I respond, "If you don't like money, don't let that keep you from setting big goals. Go earn the money and give it away if you don't like it." Whether we want to admit it or not, our world relies on resources to function, which require money. Money is not the root of all evil either. The love of money is often the root of evil, but the money itself is not. Guns don't kill people; people kill people. Money is not bad; people become bad when they are greedy for money. That's enough right now on money; let's discuss other resources like opportunity. Opportunities like money don't continue to show up for people who keep their heads in a bad spot. If you keep your head down and think about all the reasons you will never have money or opportunity, money and opportunity will fly right past you. It is said, "Opportunities don't go away; they just go to someone else."

Money is the same way. Do you see money as something that makes you arrogant, rude, or abrasive? Do you see money as the thing that makes people treat others poorly? If so, maybe you should change your perspective and see money for what it really is. Money is a tool. Like other resources, money can provide the much-needed help that people need. Healthcare costs money, food costs money, and people need both. So, if you really want to create some good resources, construct a good, healthy perspective on what the right resources could do for you and the people around you, then get to work. Also, if you get some money, give some money. Generosity can rewire how your brain sees money, and you may begin to see that there is a lot more money out there than what you first believed.

65

YOUR INFLUENCE Eventually Shrinks To The Level Of YOUR MINDSET

"Critical thought is a wonderful thing that can lead you to deeper truths."

Ronnie Doss

Blind faith is a thing of the past for people who use their brains. I understand that there will always be things we cannot explain about the universe, but I have a hard time just taking someone else's opinion as absolute truth. There is so much information in the world, and people are being exposed to new truths that obliterate old ways of thinking concerning many fundamental topics. The history of the universe, the earth, human civilization, and life forms existing in other galaxies are just a few subjects people are increasingly interested in. For me to be able to keep up, I must be willing to pay attention. Of course, not everything you see or read on the internet is true, but you can't keep reading old materials and thinking that you know everything. Sharpening your mind with new, relevant information is paramount to having influence. If the information you share is not compelling to you, it will not be compelling to your audience. Life is not all about gathering information, but it is about helping to move our species forward with technological advancements in healthcare, education, economic development, and more. Do yourself and others around you a favor; read about some new things. You may find something you're immensely passionate about, and that passion could push you toward more fulfillment and contribution. The only limits out there are the ones you've created in your mind.

Your Income Won't Grow If YOU DON'T

"I used to think the key was just to work hard. Now I know the key is to work hard at smart work."

Ronnie Doss

You can spend your whole life working hard. I enjoy hard work, but it also has its limits. When we don't innovate how we do what we do and learn to scale our abilities, we will always be working the same way: exchanging our time for dollars. Scaling your business in any way takes risk. Risks can come with a lot of payoffs and a lot of costs. Being strategic and taking calculated risks is how I have scaled my business and life overall. Investing in recording equipment, computers, editing software, renting studio space, and leasing offices in busy work areas are only a few ways I have pushed myself outside of what was comfortable. Putting on events and hiring people to create content and marketing for them is not cheap. Neither is paying the food and beverage minimums at some of the most excellent resorts in the country. I do that many times each year. All of it has helped me to grow! I have made mistakes but have also benefitted from putting myself in growth situations.

I hope you love your job. If you do, you are fortunate. But, even if you love your job, do you still think it's possible to stretch yourself in some other way to create more resources? Have you considered a "side hustle?" Doing what you must do until you can do what you want is a process. Speeding up your growth can speed up your ability to earn.

Earn, learn, return. That is the way this thing goes.

67

No Sense Of Urgency, But Living In The URGENT WILL KILL YOU

"The last minute is a good place to make good things happen only a very small percentage of the time."

Ronnie Doss

If you don't plan and prepare for what's coming, you will spend the majority of your time in a state of emergency. Panic tends to be a personality trait of those individuals who don't think and plan ahead. Have you ever been around someone who is always in a panic and a perpetual state of drama? They never have enough time, money, resources, or help to assist them in dealing with all the situations they caused with their own neglect. People who don't plan live with a "pot-of-gold mentality." They believe that somehow there will be a pot of gold they will luckily stumble upon that will save them from their irresponsibility. The problem with that type of thinking is that eventually, their luck runs out, and it comes time to pay up. Not only can poor planning cause you to waste a lot of time, but living in a panic state where everything is urgent because you're trying to make up for all the poor planning is also terrible for your health. Stress leads to many complications, and most stress is mental! When you don't plan, get your affairs in order, and then worry about it, you end up punishing yourself in very unconscious ways. There is a better way. PLAN! If something is important to you, it's worth creating a plan for. Don't get hit head-on by something you could have seen coming a mile away.

68

NEGLECT Is Like Holding A Grenade That Says, "PULL PIN IN CASE OF EMERGENCY!"

"Neglect neglect the same way you're neglecting the things you shouldn't be neglecting."

Ronnie Doss

Your health can be a ticking time bomb. Your financial status could be a ticking time bomb. A simple doctor or accountant visit can help eliminate the grenade you might be holding. Even though you have become comfortable neglecting some things, at some time or another, neglect will present the consequences to you, and they'll probably be at a really terrible time. Sweeping things under the rug eventually keeps us from being able to step without tripping. Some people are stubborn, and some are unaware, but neither can be an excuse for things that can quickly wreck the goals we have been working for. Letting drinking or drug abuse continue to exist when you know it's going to lead to disaster is a form of neglect. Not getting a handle on your spending and falling deep into debt is a form of neglect. Not having conversations about your relationship with your spouse, children, and coworkers is a form of neglect. Please hear me: the thing you are neglecting can wind up burying you if you don't take action sooner rather than later. Not to mention, the fear of impending doom for not handling the thing that could be a problem only perpetuates the problem. A clear conscience is a wonderful thing to have. It is worth more than gold. Are you neglecting something? The amount of time it has taken you to read this page in this book is longer than the amount of time it could take to make the first step toward taking the initiative. Send a text, make the call, put down this book, and do something about what you've been neglecting. If you don't know where to start, ask someone. Do it now. The best way to get out of a hole is first to put down the shovel!

69

RESISTANCE TO CHANGE
Freezes You In Time

"Glory days lead to mediocre days."

Ronnie Doss

Please do us all a favor, Uncle Rico, and stop talking about how things were in high school! Stop talking about how great things used to be. Stop talking about college, your drinking buddies, and the fraternity or sorority you used to pay to be a member of. No one cares. The stories are entertaining to you but cause many of us to feel sorry for you. Why? Because you act like the best parts of you got stuck way back when. No one cares where you used to work, how much weight you used to bench, and what they used to call you. Today is here, and there are many things we can focus on that could catapult us into a better future. While you're busy talking about when you were a big fish in a small pond, other people are building oceans where new hopes and dreams come to life every day. There is nothing wrong with remembering where you came from, but if you never leave, you have nowhere to have come from. You are stuck! You can dress up stuck with all the alcohol and humor you want, but the truth is, you're missing out by continually looking over your shoulder.

70

CULTURE Must Be
CONTINUALLY CULTIVATED

"Your family, workplace, and even your own self has a specific culture that must be cultivated. Everything rises and falls on culture, so choose it wisely."

Ronnie Doss

I'll remind you again that you are the CEO of Y-O-U Incorporated. You must make high-level decisions that affect all the organization's members, even if it's only you. All corporations have mission statements that encompass the values and purpose of their work. We must be the same! Years ago, I spoke at an event where my wife joined me at our resource table. As I was greeting people and signing books, my wife said she noticed how people approached me and addressed me. She said that how people reacted to me had changed over the years and that she could tell how much people respected me and the message that I brought. People treat us the way we teach them to treat us. Standards are part of culture. How you respect yourself, dress, take care of your physical body, and communicate with others are all parts of the standards you hold for yourself. How you behave and manage your time is another reflection of the standards you have for yourself. Do you speak clearly and confidently? Do you carry yourself well and command respect when interacting with groups or individuals? Is your appearance one that exudes casualness, or do you dress professionally and appear ready to operate on your job with excellence? These questions may seem a bit superficial, but in a world where people still judge by appearance, the standards you carry yourself with will inevitably leave a lasting impact. When it comes to standards, it's worth the work required to raise them as high as you can in as many areas as possible.

71

Relationships Can Be Messy, But HONOR And RESPECT Can Clean Them Up

"Relationships can bring you some of the most frustration you will ever experience, but they also have the potential to bring you incredible amounts of joy.
Handle them with care."

Ronnie Doss

"Honor up, honor down, honor all around." I heard a speaker share that phrase from a platform many years ago, and it stuck with me. Honor, non-judgment, and mutual respect are vital to a healthy relationship. How we relate to our family and friends, coworkers, and colleagues can significantly impact how we show honor and respect to others. Remember this always: PEOPLE WILL NOT ALWAYS MEET YOUR PREFERENCES, but you can still be kind regardless. No, you don't have to agree with other people's lifestyles and choices, but if they are not causing harm to others, then let them do their thing. It's their life; how others live their lives shouldn't steal your joy. Our society is breeding people who are so hateful and unaccepting of others that I often wonder if those things will be a reason our country could crumble. Of course, I hope not, but many great societies have crumbled from the inside due to a lack of honor and integrity. I believe they both go hand in hand. When we honor people, we treat them with integrity. We keep our word; we don't take advantage of or exploit them in any way. A lack of honor for others can weaken connections between people, and weak relationships lead to discord and disruption. Honor is the key. We can disagree, but we can also show honor to one another. Things can get ugly, but honoring someone enough to engage in a healthy dialogue and apologize when necessary can clean up mistakes made along the way.

72

Practice Won't Make You PERFECT But It Will Make You BETTER

"Perfection is an illusion that will only leave you disappointed and frustrated with reality."

Ronnie Doss

John Wooden, coach of the UCLA men's basketball team, once said, "Practice doesn't make perfect; practice only makes better." There is no such thing as perfection. It does not exist. Everything can get better with a bit of time and effort. Yes, Olympians can receive a perfect score after executing some athletic routine, but the actual idea that something is perfect is wrong. ALL things can improve. You are not perfect, your kids are not perfect, your friends are not perfect, and neither am I. Every day holds within it the opportunity to grow and improve. If we stop growing and improving, we are already finished. If a home were perfect, no one would ever need to remodel it. If an automobile were perfect, there would be no need to update its functionality and performance. The world is changing, and hopefully, it is changing for the better. Your relationships are changing, and hopefully, they are changing for the better, also. Hopefully, your health and financial status will change for the better. Things that can be measured can be improved. Perfection is a belief that often causes people to stop giving their best to an endeavor. Most people will believe they must be perfect before they can begin a new business, write a book, compose a song, or create content. As a result, they never start. Instead of thinking of yourself in terms of perfection, think of yourself as being in progress. Better will come if you can get started and stick with the process. If you stay with it long enough, you can become a leader in your field. Every professional began as an amateur. Never forget that!

73

Relationships Are MIRRORS For Us To See How We Are GROWING

"If you want to see how you're growing, ask the people who know you best."

Ronnie Doss

If your relationships are behaving just like they always have, you may not be growing as much as you think. People tend to attract and stick with people with similar spirits, confidence levels, and ambition. People who are incongruent in vision and ambition only work together well for a short time. Opposites can indeed attract, but the differences should help to balance one another out, not weigh one another down. My wife and I have been together for twenty years. We have different strengths and gifts; mine tend to be much more outgoing and aggressive. She tends to be calmer and more patient, especially regarding how we raised our children when they were younger. Our differences have balanced us out. I would not want to be married to me. That would be a disaster. We use humor, honor, and honesty as the foundation for our relationship. When something needs to be talked about, we talk about it. The difference between us and relationships that don't work is that our conversations are wrapped in honor and respect, even if we disagree. Relationships are never without challenges. Even the best relationships hit obstacles and roadblocks at times. However, how two people address the challenges reflects their maturity and wisdom. Age doesn't mean maturity; how we handle responsibility is a reflection of maturity. When you mature, the relationships you are in mature as well. If they don't, those relationships may not be for you. Never be afraid of going for long walks alone when honor, honesty, and respect are not being served.

74

Be INTERESTED, Not Just INTERESTING

"It's nice to be the most interesting person in the room, but it does no good if the people listening to you think you're condescending and obnoxious."

Ronnie Doss

Have you ever shared a story that was important to you only to have someone else "one up" you? People who continually do that are not genuinely concerned with how you feel; they are more concerned with how they look. Insecure people overcompensate with larger-than-life stories, exaggerated claims, negative perspectives, and ridicule of anyone or anything that might outdo them. I love to talk, and I have built an extraordinary career doing it. I read a lot and listen to insightful books, podcasts, and lectures. I probably consume more information than a large majority of the population. I do it not to impress people but to sharpen my mind and strengthen my brain.

When I feel confident in myself and my mind is sharp, I notice that I don't need to talk about myself. The more confident I feel, the better questions I ask. When you learn to ask good questions, people will tell you things about them that matter to them. When people feel listened to and valued, they feel better about themselves. When we can become the person who makes others feel good about themselves, it makes everything around us better. We can learn to encourage people to what their next level is. The next time you are with someone, give them your undivided attention and ask heartfelt questions. You will be surprised at what you can learn and how you can make someone feel. Maya Angelou said, *"I have learned that people will forget what you said, people will forget what you did, but people will never forget how you made them feel."* Carry this idea with you into every conversation, and things will go well for you.

75

Success Is Not About BEING THE BEST; It's About Working To BE YOUR BEST

"Be better than you were yesterday. If you can do that again and again, who's the best will take care of itself."

Ronnie Doss

You know who you are. You know how much effort you give. You know what goals you are compelled to achieve, and you know whether or not you are giving your best. Success is maximizing what has been gifted to you in the form of talent and ability. You may need to gain the talent to play in the NBA, but if you want to improve on your jump shot and be able to hit ten free throws in a row, only you can do the work necessary to practice. Success is personal. Becoming the best version of you has nothing to do with whether other people are becoming the best versions of themselves. If you want to be the best, be the best example of effort. Some musicians are born with an ear for music. Many artists are born with the ability to see an object and reproduce an image on a canvas with little effort. However, most of us are not born with those talents. We must work extremely hard to refine the process. I am outgoing, but that doesn't make me a great communicator. For me to get better at communicating ideas and concepts, I record and listen to myself when I am in front of an audience. Learning to change my pitch, volume, speed, and cadence of how I deliver content has made me better and better over the years. Still, I have work to do. I am working to be my best, not the best. I am not comparing myself to others because I do not care what others are doing. Hopefully, they are sharing their passions with the world in a way that exemplifies their best efforts. When you stop looking outside of yourself for answers and look within, you will find that the answer to success lies within you. You hold the key. Be your best. Practice as much as you can. Get serious about what you do and hold yourself accountable. This is the recipe for success!

76

Your LIMITATIONS Are Rooted In The Soil Of YOUR BELIEFS

"The idea that you could be wrong about who you are is an exciting thing."

Ronnie Doss

Your job doesn't define you. Your family status doesn't define you. Society doesn't define you. Your results don't define you. YOU define you. And, every day, you have the chance to redefine yourself and how you do your life. When someone says, "Well, this is just the way I have always been." I say to myself, "So?!" Who you believe you are is a collection of events, interpretations, conversations, traumas, dramas, and victories. You make up the story. I learned many years ago that the FACTS DO NOT MATTER when it comes to what we make something mean. Yes, there are natural responses to events, especially traumatic ones. However, you and I have the power and ability to make up any story we want about any situation we find ourselves in.

Even the most traumatic circumstances can be interpreted in a way that compels us to take positive action. I have dear friends who have lost children in automobile accidents. It's one of the worst things that could happen to parents. However, my friends decided to use the pain as a catalyst for helping others deal with life's difficulties. They did not quit; they did not become bitter and resentful; they carried on. If they had allowed themselves to believe that their loss was the end of the world, they could have easily thrown in the towel and given up on life. Instead, they began the healing process by digging deep within their hearts and minds and leaned into the love and support they had from family and friends around them. Just because you feel it doesn't mean that your perspective is reality. You can change your life by confronting beliefs that do not serve you. Every time you take action toward something new, you fire and rewire neuropathways in your brain. Over time, you can redesign your beliefs and shatter old limitations. It takes work, but it is better than allowing some limiting belief to hold you back.

77

MOVE FORWARD In The Direction Of Your Goal With Such Power That It Creates A Force That PULLS PEOPLE To Their NEXT LEVEL

"Don't wait for the light at the end of the tunnel; be the light at the beginning of the tunnel."

Ronnie Doss

Have you ever been around someone so passionate about what they were talking about that it excited you, too? When someone talks about a great movie they saw, a great book they read, or a great concert they attended, their enthusiasm becomes contagious. I mentioned earlier in the book that passion is the great persuader. If you want someone to follow you, you must have passion for the journey as well as the destination. Passion can shift people's attitudes, increase their energy, and improve their morale. Passionate people have a much greater chance of getting people involved with their cause than those who come off as lukewarm. People respond to an exciting vision quicker than they do an exhaustive need. The next time you want to persuade someone to get on board with your cause, extract as much information as possible about the particular thing you are discussing and get excited about the details and possibilities. The world doesn't need more people; the world needs more people to come alive with passion. Get excited, write out an exciting plan, get excited about the plan, and then take massive action. Once the train starts rolling, it might take you places you've never dreamed of. But you must start somewhere.

78

We Are Each Responsible For How Our Actions IMPACT ALL OF US

"Every choice we make impacts more than just what we see with our own eyes."

Ronnie Doss

When you think of your family and team, do you see them as allies or enemies? Do you see them as comrades or competition? People who see everyone as competition rarely live a harmonious life. To be a part of a healthy group, we must learn to care for ourselves. What good does it do to love someone but never be able to help them out in their time of need? What good is it to want to be there for your children as they grow older but allow your health to diminish completely? Yes, things happen, and we do get sick. But, living a lifestyle that is destructive to you ends up affecting the other people that you are so closely connected to. If you allow yourself to fall into unhealthy addictions, abusive relationships, or bad financial positions, it can put pressure on the people who care about you most. If you genuinely love people, start by taking really good care of yourself and the things you can control. Eat well, move well, think well, and things will tend to go well for you. When things go well for you, you will be in a much better place to help others when they need it. Hopefully, if you are ever in a place where you need help, the people who care about you are in a good enough position to assist you. Life is not all about you, but if you don't take care of yourself, there won't be much life for you to give.

79

When You Get It, GIVE IT
When You Learn It, TEACH IT

"When it comes to energy and resources, the buck must not stop here. Keep it moving!"

Ronnie Doss

Water that stops moving becomes stagnant and filled with harmful bacteria. Water that keeps moving stays cleaner. Energy works much the same way, just as resources do. When we hoard money, resources, knowledge, and ideas, everything stops with us. Many people will keep great ideas to themselves, hold back from sharing their talents with others, and essentially miss opportunities to make their team and the world around them better. When we recognize that we are not the center of the universe and that there is nothing new under the sun, we are grateful for what we have and are willing to share it. Stingy people rarely do anything compelling. Stingy people typically wind up unhealthy with unhealthy relationships around them because they have an unhealthy relationship with energy. Energy must keep moving for it to have a positive effect on its environment. You are energy. Your body produces enough energy at any given moment to power a 100-watt light bulb. In some instances, it only takes a couple of hundred watts of energy to power a laser that can cut through steel. You are a force to be reckoned with. Take what you know, think of it as energy, and let it flow. Share what you learn. Share what you receive. Don't be stingy. The more you release, the more you have room to receive.

80

You Don't Get What You WANT; You Get What You're COMMITTED TO

"What you want and what you do about it have absolutely nothing to do with each other."

Ronnie Doss

Kids tell Santa what they want for Christmas; that's about all they have to do when it comes to receiving from Ol' Saint Nick. However, they do have to stay off the naughty list if they want to get the gifts. Life is much the same way. Our behavior does determine what we end up with. Bad things appear under your life's Christmas tree if you act badly. Poor thinking, negative attitudes, and a lack of self-discipline can bring us "gifts" that we probably won't be excited about. Santa only comes once each year, but consequences can show up any day at any time. Throughout our lives, if our behavior causes harm to ourselves or others, eventually, we will have to pay for it. As one of my friends says, "Karma is a real A-hole." When I began working for my mentor 15 years ago, he taught me that everyone wanted nice things. He said that many people believed that wanting to be a good person made them a good person. But there is more to being a good person than simply having good intentions. To be a good person, we must act like a good person. People must be able to see our goodness, not just hear it from our mouths. If you hired someone to follow you around for a week, would they be able to see that you were truly committed to your goals, or would they just be able to see that you are committed to talking about your goals? Turn off the audio regarding your goals, and turn on the video. Watch how you show up, not just how you talk about showing up. They are as far apart as the East is from the West. Don't be fooled; talk is cheap.

81

A Wise Man SPEAKS LESS And CONTRIBUTES MORE. A Fool SPEAKS CONTINUALLY And ADDS LITTLE

"Speak less; they listen more."

Ronnie Doss

A friend once told me that the loudest person in the room was the most insecure in the room. I have found that to be true over the years. If you want something done, give it to the person who talks the least. After a decade of speaking to corporations, businesses, non-profits, and individuals, I understand the power of words. But, if those words are not weighed and carefully thought out, they can lose their power to impact and can unintentionally damage a person or group of people. How you say what you say is as important as what you say. Think about the difference in saying, "What's bothering you?" Versus saying, "What's wrong with you?" The context may have intended to mean the same thing, but the interpretation will be very different. Consider your words well. Think of what it would feel like to hear someone say to you some of the things you say to others. Do your words encourage and lift people's spirits, or are you a passive-aggressive person who uses your words to keep people down? My mother always said, "If you don't have something nice to say, don't say anything at all." To me, that is wisdom. The better you get with your vocabulary and abilities to convey it, the better the opportunities that will come your way. Author Brian Tracy once told me, "The better you can compel a board room to take action, the better your income will be."

82

Everyone That Is WITH YOU Is NOT FOR YOU, And Everyone That Is FOR YOU Is NOT WITH YOU

"Not everyone deserves a seat on your life bus."

Ronnie Doss

On a Facebook personal page, you can have up to 5,000 friends. Wow! That's actually a lot of friends. If you want to find out how many of those people are really your friends, ask them to send you five dollars and see what happens. Friends, acquaintances, colleagues, and so on are not the same thing. Friends are the people that will be there for you regardless of the storm you are in. Fair-weather friends will be there as long as it's convenient and beneficial for them. Secret haters will act like your friends, but behind your back, hope you'll fail. I have friends around the world, and I am very proud of the relationships I have. Relationships must be cared for. Relationships must be protected. Relationships must be valued. In a world where we can see so many people on our electronic devices, it's easy to stop engaging with those closest to us. I try to reach out to at least one person I care about daily and encourage them. I could do more, but I feel good about how I personally create and maintain healthy relationships. Get a stack of blank cards, write a note to someone you love each day, and drop it in the mail. It will be a nice surprise for them and make you feel good too. Relationships are the key to the door that leads to joy and satisfaction. Don't overlook the beautiful relationships you have around you, and do a little extra work to make them better. It's worth it!

83

Until The ACID OF PAIN Eats Through Your COCOON OF DENIAL, You Won't CHANGE

"You may not believe in potholes, but you're going to get a flat tire when you hit one that is deep enough."

Ronnie Doss

Failure hurts, loss hurts, breakups hurt. Many things that hurt us in life could be avoided with just a little honesty. You don't have to wait for tragedy to set in before you start making some changes to your life. You don't have to wait until your spouse walks out on you before you treat them better. You don't have to wait until your kids stop speaking to you to start making an effort to develop the relationship in a healthier way. Often, PAIN is spelled W-A-I-T. If you continue to wait to do what you know needs to be done, pain is going to slam into you like a wave off the coast of Hawaii. I have worked with teams that had their entire staff walk out on them. I have worked with people who have had their spouses abandon them in the middle of the night. The waiting game doesn't pay off when it comes to priorities.

Unless you are a glutton for punishment, you may need to be honest about your life. If you've been putting off having a tough conversation with your spouse, boss, or friend, it's time to do something about it. If you've been waiting to see the doctor about a health issue, it's time to do something about it. If you've been acting like a child and taking out your emotional tantrums on the people you care about, you may need to apologize and change your ways. Things don't get better naturally; things get better intentionally. Go ahead and pull off the bandaid and heal the wound. Otherwise, you'll die the death of a thousand little cuts. Grow up! It matters.

84

Honey Badgers Aren't Concerned With The Opinions Of. . . ANYONE

"Not everything is worthy of a response from you."

Ronnie Doss

The higher you go, the louder the voices of criticism seem to get. People are mean, rude, and inconsiderate at times. That said, how other people think of you is really none of your business. People will judge you, hate on you, and talk about you. This is life. Put on a hard hat and get back to work. I used to think that people talking about me was a bad thing. Now, I realize you probably aren't doing much if people are not talking about you. There is a story in the Bible where Jesus was hanging on the cross dying, and he said, "Father, forgive them, for they know not what they do." At such a terrible time in Jesus' life, he still asked God to forgive them because he realized how foolish people can be. This is not meant to be a religious lesson but a simple life lesson. People are foolish, but that doesn't mean we have to respond in foolish ways. When we can rise above the opinions of others with optimism and compassion, we separate ourselves from the grip of the grabs that are trying to pull us down. If you want more influence, you will have to deal with more ignorance. They go hand in hand. We are part of humanity but don't have to act like them. I believe we are responsible for behaving better than the society we grew up in. Rise up until you get all the way up. Keep climbing even when they try to get you down. They are not going where you are, and that's okay.

85

Your FRIEND'S BUSINESS Is Not Your OTHER FRIEND'S BUSINESS

"If you can't keep a secret, you won't be able to keep friends either."

Ronnie Doss

If a person values you enough to share a secret with you, keep it. I've heard it said that you will know you have a friend when they have the tools to destroy you but refuse to." Consulting with businesses the way I do, I learn things about people, employers, and employees that could cause me to be highly judgmental of them. Though my natural impulse is to pass judgment, I remind myself that I can do my job in a much more effective way if I can remain dispassionate about the particular incident and look at the situation through an unbiased lens. When you are privy to information that could harm others, it is your responsibility to handle that information respectfully. Knowing something about a situation others may not know can put you in an odd predicament. However, loose lips sink ships. You don't have to tell everything you know, and you shouldn't have to name-drop to get invited into certain circles. People want a friend. We all want someone we know we can count on. When people confide in me, I keep it to myself. There are many times I don't even tell my wife what I know about people because I don't believe it positively impacts how she sees them. There is no need to bring her into the mess if there is one. If someone lets you know about something that is a potential threat to the well-being of others, then you have a responsibility to speak up. Otherwise, keep secrets. Don't throw other people under the bus because there is always a bus headed in your direction as well. You reap what you sow; don't forget that.

86

Service Doesn't Make You A SERVANT

"Opening the door for others doesn't make you a doormat. Be polite and keep a smile on your face."

Ronnie Doss

Have you ever opened the door for someone and they didn't say "thank you?" How did you feel? Did it upset you? If so, have you ever considered that you weren't opening the door for them; you were opening the door for a response? It is an interesting thing to consider. Are we doing nice things for people because we care about them, or are we doing nice things for them so that people will think we are a nice person? They are not the same thing! I host events for groups of entrepreneurs a few times a year. I love the group, and we all learn so much from each other when we are together. The group is called Tribe. During those events, we eat a lot and have cigars, and some of the guys enjoy having a glass of bourbon while they sit together in the evening and discuss life. While the guys are spending time connecting, I am constantly cleaning up and making sure everyone has what they need. I do it as a labor of love. It's my way of contributing to the guys' experience and ensuring things run smoothly. I am happy to serve, but that doesn't make me a servant. It simply expresses who I choose to be: a leader.

If serving is beneath you, leadership is far above you. Be willing to take someone's plate after they have finished their meal. Pick up some trash if you see it lying around. Do your part to serve, and maybe others will see you and choose to do the same. If they don't, that's okay too. You're not doing it to make people do anything; you're doing it because that's who you choose to be. The greatest leaders have the position they do because they learned to serve right where they were, and it opened doors for them.

87

Be Careful Of Who You Allow To DESCRIBE YOU TO YOU

"If you allow the noise of other people's opinions to remain in your mind, you won't be able to hear the most important opinion of all: yours!"

Ronnie Doss

I don't let people's words stick to me. I pay them no attention if their words don't align with where I am going. It hasn't always been that way. At the beginning of my career, I was concerned with how people perceived me. Over time, though, I stopped worrying about what people thought of me by being consistent and giving my all to the events I was doing. The results were clear: I was delivering a good product. I am not insinuating that people should be delusional and oblivious when it comes to not worrying about the opinions of others. I simply mean that one shouldn't put so much value into what others say. People say stupid things, and people don't know the whole story. If you are working hard and your heart is in the right spot, keep working hard, and good things will come your way. Martin Luther King Jr. said, "It's not what people call you that matters; what matters is what you answer to." What do you answer to? If you see yourself as a winner, then don't spend time around people who would try to speak to you as if you were a loser. If people take shots at you with their comments, let them know that you aren't going to bless them with your presence if they disrespect you. Don't be afraid of saying, "I warned you once. I won't do it again." People will respect you to the level you respect yourself. Words are powerful. Use them well and ignore the people that don't.

88

There's A Difference Between BUILDING PEOPLE And Using People To BUILD AN AGENDA

"Good people make other people feel good. They encourage, uplift, and leave people in a better spot than where they found them. Leaders build people up."

Ronnie Doss

Getting people to buy into your cause will require them to believe in you. However, it is not all about you. It must be about the people who are following you. Thinking only of yourself will lead people off a cliff if it means you benefit. But, if you are genuinely concerned with helping people improve the quality of their lives, you do whatever you can to assist them as often as possible. The larger your organization, the less personal time you will have for each person, but by keeping the best interests of your team as the highest priority, the team will be able to endure the challenges that come with working together. So many times, I have seen organizations that have fallen apart because the leader exploited the group members and never catered to anything they needed. Leaders don't stand up front. Leaders lead from all positions, even if it means from behind. The leader's vision compels the group to take action, but the leader's willingness to do the work also pushes the group forward. It requires both vision and contribution. The best leaders step off the platform, serve alongside the group, and march forward alongside the other team members. Don't think of yourself too highly if you are in a lead position. Humble yourself and lock arms with the people marching for the cause. You will go much further than you would have walking alone.

89

If You Don't Like Something, Take Away What Gives It Power...
YOUR ATTENTION

"What you focus on expands, and what you ignore tends to go away. What you focus on determines where and how you arrive."

Ronnie Doss

The celebrity "code" is, *"Never read the comments."* What the "code" references are the comments that people make about them on social media platforms. Some of the most wicked and insensitive things ever written were by losers sitting in their parent's basement with nothing else to do other than criticize the people making things happen. The more you remember this, the less attention you will give to the words written by keyboard warriors. You can post the greatest thing about something you feel incredibly proud of, and inevitably, someone will have something rude to say about it. Ignore it! Laugh at it! Think about it for a moment. What kind of person sits and types out criticisms of other people's lives? Is it a happy person? Is it a person who is busy doing great things for our world? Is it someone that wants other people to win? No! Of course not. People who say negative things only express the pain and stupidity they must go to bed with every night. Hurting people try to hurt people. Don't fall for it. You have too many good things to think about and create. Don't give your valuable attention to people that don't carry much value.

90

The Only Control You Have Over TOMORROW Is The Seeds You Plant TODAY

"What you do today will determine what you can do tomorrow."

Ronnie Doss

When holding a seed in your hand, it is the biggest it will ever be. When you sow the seed, it is the smallest it will ever be. You must build your future by laying the groundwork today. The one thing about tomorrow is that it always shows up. When you plant seeds in the ground, it doesn't do any good to sit beside where you planted them, yelling at them to hurry up and grow. The best thing you can do is plant the seed and then plant some more. The best time to plant a tree was thirty years ago and today. You hold so many seeds in your hands at any time. Seeds of love, compassion, knowledge, and contribution are beautiful things to sow in a world that needs all the good things it can get. Think of yourself as a distributor of seeds, and the universe will eventually reward you with excellent fruit. You reap what you sow, not what you intended to sow. So, get to work. And lastly, once you've sown seeds, don't forget to water the seeds. I mean, be willing to go back and inspect what's going on with the seeds you've sown. Check back with people and follow up to see how they are doing. As you continue to water the seeds, healthy things will eventually grow. A whole forest lies within one acorn. See your talents and abilities as the acorn that must be planted in the hearts and minds of others. Powerful things can grow to extraordinary heights because you are willing to do your part.

91

Tired Eyes Rarely See
ANYTHING COMPELLING

"When I'm tired, I play the quiet game with myself because I usually don't have anything good to say."

Ronnie Doss

Have you ever spent a whole day painting a room? You covered the trim, taped off the electrical outlets, put the plastic on the floor, and went to work. After a long day of putting paint on the walls, it's easy to be critical of your work. However, if you can just put the lid on the paint can and return to the room the following day after a good night's rest, the room will appear totally different. It's the same room, color, and trim, but it looks much better than when you were exhausted the night before. This is true for so many other instances in life. When we are exhausted and our brain has run out of all the "goodies," we can be incredibly critical of things. Giving yourself time to unplug, rest, and recalibrate can give you the proper perspective on what you are looking at. Projects, people, and opportunities can all appear very different when we are rested and have fresh eyes. Have you ever had your phone or computer start to behave oddly? The solution is often to unplug it or turn it off. The same is true for us! Sometimes, the best way to solve a problem is to walk away from it for a while and approach it again with a new mind. A few steps, breaths, and a little rest can make all the difference in the world. If you're tapped out, do yourself a favor and practice quieting your mind.

92

PATIENCE Is A Weapon That Causes DECEPTION To REVEAL ITSELF

"Give things a little time and you'll begin to see them for what they really are."

Ronnie Doss

Have you ever felt so compelled to buy something that you completely overlooked the contract's fine print? Emotion can blind us from specifics. We tend to see what we want to see. There is a term called "camp goggles." This is where you act as if you are at camp, much like when you were younger and saw someone who was sort of cute. Because there may not have been many people to choose from at the camp, the "camp goggles" caused you to magnify any of the positive attributes you might have seen as attractive and minimized the things you didn't like. When we rush to make things happen, we can slip on the old camp goggles and pretend not to see things that might deter us from taking action. For example, learning to be patient is one of the most valuable things you can do to have peace of mind and make quality purchases. You'd be amazed at how much money you can usually save when you are willing to walk away and sleep on the limited-time offer. Limited-time offers typically get extended, and the price tends to lower. I recently had this happen on a pretty expensive contract I just signed. I saved nearly 25 percent of the purchase price by holding out and not rushing. Patience is your friend. Learn to live with it, and you won't have to live with as many erroneous, impulsive decisions.

93

People Respond To VISION Quicker Than NEED

"People are more willing to get on board a ship that is sailing somewhere tropical than they are one that's headed toward the rocks."

Ronnie Doss

If you want to get your family or team on board with an idea, you must identify and explain the benefits of joining the movement. Whether it's a big project, a small project, or just a simple request, getting people excited about it will make all the difference. When working with sales teams, I remind them that people always listen to things on their personal radio station. **W-I-I-F-M**. **W**hat's **I**n **I**t **F**or **M**e? This is the question they are asking. If you can get them excited about the potential payoff, they will be much more prone to get involved. If you need some extra cash, come up with something that you can do to reward the person who loans you some money. Don't just pay them back; offer an even greater solution. When we move into a needy place, the energy we put off can repel people from wanting to help us out. Make your vision exciting, and people will come running. Use this with your children, also. Reward them if they get good grades or achieve a great accomplishment. I just spoke with a friend who is taking his daughter to a resort in Mexico because she hit a personal goal. Make it exciting, make it compelling, and magical things can happen! Add some pizzazz to your request, and watch the positive responses increase! If you can make them say "wow," you can make them say "yes!"

94

If You Want To Be PROMOTED To The Next Level, You Must Become OVERQUALIFIED For The Level You're At

---

"If you're going to ask for more, you must be able to deliver more."

Ronnie Doss

Why should an employer or customer pay you more for something they can get someone else to do for the same price? It's easy to become the ME MONSTER and see things only from your perspective. However, the world doesn't see things the way you do. The world doesn't see you as valuable as you see yourself. The world sees you only as valuable as the goods you can deliver. While working for him many years ago, I approached my mentor once and said, "I would like a raise." He looked at me and said some words I have never forgotten. He looked me straight in the eyes and said, "If you want a raise, solve a problem you aren't already solving. I'm not just going to give you a raise because you think you deserve one." Now that I have people who work with me, I won't pay them more just because they might want it. I pay for the value they are bringing to the team. If you want to be paid on a higher level, think and solve problems on a higher level. Otherwise, you will earn what you already earn for the rest of your life.

95

CHANTING And PLANTING Are Not The Same Thing

"Speaking positively without taking positive action is the beginning of delusion."

Ronnie Doss

You can name it and claim it all you want, but that doesn't mean good things will just come your way. You can tear your knees up, begging the universe to give you something, but you will be lacking most of your life if you aren't willing to stand up and take massive action. I have known people who truly believed God would give them things without even having to work for them. I have known people so indoctrinated with a "prosperity" gospel that they believed their words were the only seeds they had to sow. Talking won't get you to places where only walking can take you. Yes, speak positively, but let me make something very clear: if you don't work for it, you don't deserve it. Easy come, easy go.

People who do the work when no one is looking are the ones stretching their capacity for good things to happen. The people who are good stewards of their resources and are willing to invest in wise things are the ones that the universe rewards. Run from people who think all you have to do is speak it, and it will manifest. Those people are delusional and dangerous. Let your walk be just as compelling as your talk; soon enough, rewards will make their way to you. Get ready!

96

WITHOUT ACTION, You Can Begin To RESENT POSSIBILITIES

"If you won't take some risks and seize the chance, you will eventually get frustrated with yourself and blame the opportunity for it."

Ronnie Doss

It doesn't take much to be a coward. My mentor used to say, "People who know what to do and do nothing are worse people than the ones who don't know what to do at all." If you look around and don't like what you see, change it. Ask your spouse, "Is there something about our lives together that you want to improve?" Don't get mad when they are honest with you. They are just giving you feedback. Feedback is the breakfast of champions. If you don't like feedback, you won't like the results you produce. A great question to ask is, "What needs to change around me, and who do I need to become to do that?" If you don't like where you live, move! You're not a tree. If you can't move, figure out a plan, develop a strategy, and stick with it until you can. Stop settling for less because it's all you've ever known. If you are honest with yourself and don't like something about you, remember that no fairy is going to show up and sprinkle magic dust on your shoulder. You are going to have to make the change happen yourself. If you don't like where you work, find another job. If you don't like your car, trade it. If you don't like your clothes, buy some new ones. This is your life, and you decide what you're willing to settle for. At the end of your life, I don't think you'll regret the things you chose to do. I believe we will all regret what we wanted to do but didn't.

97

ONE STEP At A Time Moves You Up The STAIRCASE

"It's the small steps that lead to the biggest leaps."

Ronnie Doss

Life is a game of numbers. You can't get to two without first dealing with one. You can't make millions until you've learned to make thousands. People these days are in such a hurry to get to the top of the mountain that they forget there is a mountain to climb. You must do it one step at a time when climbing a mountain. If not, you can fall and hurt yourself. I can look back at my career and see how one small step led me to another and how one small door led me to a bigger one. I always say, *"You never know who is watching you, so give your best."* Some of the smallest audiences I have spoken to have had people in them that eventually led me to the highest-paying opportunities. This is why I said earlier in the book, *"Always be willing to get up, dress up, and show up because you never know what can happen when you do."* Forget the staircase; focus on the stairs in front of you. Pay attention so you don't stumble and miss something that could move you to the top with more wisdom. One step at a time makes for a beautiful dance.

98

Don't Be Afraid Of The Dirt; It's Where The MIRACLES ARE BURIED

"Whether it's just beneath the surface or a long way down, you're going to have to dig for all the valuable resources you want."

Ronnie Doss

The second book I wrote was titled "DIG." I used the book to explain the depths of our minds and hearts and how we must be willing to dig beyond surface-level conversations to deepen our relationships. The book is an easy read, but the truths found within it carry a lot of weight. In the movie "Bruce Almighty," Morgan Freeman plays God. In one scene, he explains to Bruce, played by Jim Carrey, that some of the happiest people on earth come home tired and dirty every night after a long day's work. It is a powerful scene with a beautiful message. The most beautiful things we can attain often come with the greatest amount of work. A great relationship with our parents or spouse takes digging. A strong relationship with our children involves digging. Most things of value aren't just lying around on the surface; if they were, they wouldn't be so valuable because everyone would have them. Digging deep and finding your purpose is the beginning of a miraculous transformation in your life. Digging past your old beliefs about yourself and the world can lead to the most beautiful manifestations. Digging beyond comfort and finding the fire in your belly can be the very thing you need to push your body back into shape. And if I may, having a deeper relationship with your creator requires digging past your intellect and stepping into faith. Maybe this book represents a type of digging for you. These insights are nudging you to believe it's time to dig a grave for the old things buried within and holding you back so you can give room to the beautiful things coming your way. Maybe you weren't just covered with dirt at times; perhaps you were planted, and now is the time for things to begin growing like never before.

99

Prefer The PAIN OF GROWTH Versus The WET BLANKET OF NEGLECT

"No part of personal growth is easy, but we don't have to make it harder than it needs to be."

Ronnie Doss

To grow, you're going to have to stretch. Stretching hurts! Growth hurts, but so does staying the same year after year. Refusing to change is ultimately saying to the universe that you are done. Feeling like you must keep going after you are done will feel like complete misery. There is no point! There is opportunity all around us: opportunities to grow, opportunities to serve, opportunities to learn, and opportunities to contribute. You are nowhere near complete. Today is the first day of the rest of your life. Today can be just "one day," or it can be DAY ONE! It can be the first day of a renewed perspective and a clearer outlook. Today can be that day. You have only just begun to see all the beauty of this life if you are willing to open your eyes wide and let it in. Maybe you start today by apologizing to yourself for the wrongs you've done and say "Thank you" for all the good you've done to get here. As you move forward, remove the wet blanket of neglect and put on the shield of faith. Pick up the sword of the spirit, and go fight for what is yours. Fight for your life, family, friends, and future. You are worth the work!

100

It Ain't Over Until You SAY IT'S OVER, And Even Then, IT'S NOT OVER

"If you can get up and will yourself past your emotions just one more time, you can accomplish anything today."

Ronnie Doss

Before picking this book up, you might have believed your potential was gone. You may have thought that you had peaked already and that the best days of your life were already gone. You might still be struggling with some sadness or depression because life hasn't turned out quite the way you'd hoped. I understand. Writing this book represents a new season for me. The season I am coming out of has been one of my life's darkest and most challenging. With so many beautiful things to be grateful for, I was still struggling to find my purpose and step into the possibility of more. Even with all the books I've read and motivational speeches I have listened to, I felt like I was floundering at times. Even with all my wonderful friends surrounding and supporting me, I still felt alone at times. Thankfully, I didn't give up. Thankfully, my wife and children continued to love me and encouraged me to keep going. As a result, here we are. I thought it might be over, but it's not. This is only the beginning.

Eleanor Roosevelt said, "The future belongs to those who believe in the beauty of their dreams." Don't give up the dreams you've dreamed, the visions you've seen just because it's taken some time to get here. One connection, encounter, and conversation can change everything for you. I believe in you! You have what it takes. Don't give up, and don't give in. Thank you for being part of this journey with me. I hope it has been as impactful for you as you have read it as it has been for me to share it. This was my gift to both of us.

101

KEEP IT MOVING!

"You may be able to fit in everywhere, but you may not feel settled anywhere. So, keep it moving!"

Ronnie Doss

Life is a collection of thoughts, memories, and actions. When you aren't sure, keep moving. When you don't feel like doing anything, move your body. When you aren't sure where to go, take some steps, and you will find out. Remember, you are winning or learning, and that's what life is about. Your gifts and talents will open many doors for you and lead you to exciting places. However, you may not feel like any of them are your permanent home. Don't get upset if you haven't arrived yet; none of us have. Everyone is on their own journey, and the journey isn't finished until you are. Keep the faith, keep your peace, and keep moving. There are far greater things ahead of you than anything behind you. One day at a time, one step at a time, you will succeed if you just don't quit. Keep moving, keep moving, keep moving. Your path is revealing itself to you every single day. God wants to bless you; just let Him do it!

Thank You

In conclusion, I would like to express my heartfelt gratitude to you for embarking on this intellectual journey through the pages of "Colossal Considerations." Your time and attention are truly appreciated. I hope that the ideas and perspectives shared within these chapters have sparked new thoughts and reflections within you.

As you continue to explore the rich tapestry of knowledge and insight presented in this book, I invite you to delve deeper into related topics and expand your understanding through other resources I have crafted. Whether it be additional writings, online courses, or interactive workshops, there is much more to discover and learn.

Please visit www.RonnieDoss.com for more.

Thank you once again for your support and engagement. May the wisdom gleaned from "Colossal Considerations" continue to resonate with you in your ongoing quest for knowledge and growth. Happy exploring!

Ronnie Doss

Notes

Colossal Consideration

Notes

Notes

Colossal Consideration

Notes

Ronnie Doss

Notes